Now What Do I Do???

A Mother's Journey
Through the Juvenile and Criminal Justice
System in America

Lisa Blumenberg

Published by Blumenberg Books

Publishing Company

Copyright 2018

Library of Congress Control Number:2019910671

ISBN 978-0-9997925-1-3

Printed in the United States of America

Book cover photographer

By Richard Ross

Thank you for buying an authorized edition of this book. In addition, thank you for complying with copyright laws by not reproducing, scanning, or distributing any part of it in any form without permission. By doing so, you are supporting authors and allowing Blumenberg Books to continue to publish books for every reader.

While the author has made every effort to provide accurate telephone numbers, Internet addresses, and other contact information at the time of publication, neither the publisher nor the author assumes any responsibilities for errors, or for changes that occur after publication. Further, the publisher does not have any control over and does not assume any responsibility for author or third-party websites or their content.

Noah's Disclaimer of Authorization:

I give Lisa Blumenberg, full authorization to write her book under conditions that I am not quoted, no personal notes are shared, any self-incriminating information is shared, and it is constantly stated that my beliefs, words and actions in the book are under her interpretation and that they are just by opinion, not fact. Also, I would like that it be included that I had no part in the writing, editing or producing of the book.

The birthing of this book was assisted by:

The Literary Midwife

Helping you get your book from your heart to your reader's hands.
www.hagarfoh.org/literary-midwife

Acknowledgements

"To God be the Glory"

This book is dedicated to my children

Brittany, Noah, and Eve

and to my Auntie Barbara Blumenberg

Thank you for being my rock.

I miss you.

Contents

Preface 1

Introduction 3

Chapter 1: I Need Help! 7

Chapter 2: The Miranda Warning 21

    1: You Have The Right To Remain Silent!!!! 24

    2: "Anything" You Say Can And Will Be Used Against You. 27

    3: You Have A Right To An Attorney… 29

    4: "And If You Don't Have An Attorney, One Will Be Assigned To You". 30

    5: Do You Understand The Rights That I Have Just Read To You? With These Rights In Mind, Do You Wish To Speak To Me? 32

Chapter 3: Questions For The Authorities 37

    God Needed To Get His Attention 44

    Time To Regroup - Everything Happens For A Reason .. 50

Chapter 4: Let The Court Hearings Begin 55

    Released With An Ankle Bracelet 59

Chapter 5: Anger 65

Chapter 6: This Time It Felt Different 77

    P – Pray 84

    R – Do Your Own Research 87

    A - Assess Confidants To Identify Your Support System 90

    Yield - Contact Your Attorney 93

Chapter 7: Questions For The Public Defender 97

Chapter 8: Penalties: Felony vs. Misdemeanor 113

    Trust Changes Your Perspective 124

Chapter 9: The Cost Of Prison 127

Chapter 10: Release 139

Chapter 11: Beware Of The Traps 147

    Trap #1: Probation 151

    Trap #2: Meetings With The Probation Officer (PO) 156

    Trap #3: Working Off-Site 156

    Trap #4: Department Of Corrections Listed On His Credit Report 157

Chapter 12: Thank Him In Advance For The Deliverance. 161

    Start Thanking Him For How He's Going To Use This Circumstance To Turn Things Around 169

Chapter 13: Spiritual Warfare 173

Chapter 14: Lessons Learned 185

Chapter15: It's Time to Dance 201

References: 211

Preface

The worst part of this experience for me was the beginning, finding out that my son wouldn't be coming home for an unknown extended period of time. I was totally oblivious to the juvenile and criminal justice system, what it meant for me and my family but most importantly, what it meant for my son. I never thought I would be in that number to have to experience what it felt like to have my child incarcerated. I wanted so much more and so much better for him in my mind; excelling and doing well is where I always saw him. I did not understand what God was doing. Through this experience, I learned that God still had the power to turn things around and all that I wanted for my son could still manifest in God's due timing. I learned that God still has the last say and it's not over until He says it's over. I still have to remind myself of this even today and to remember, that as long as my son has breath in his body, God has the final say, not the judge.

If you find yourself in this position on any level, I encourage you to never underestimate God's strength and to know that you are stronger than you think, particularly when you feel like you have no strength left. The weight of it all can make you feel like you are in a zombie-like state of mind, just

Preface

going through the motions because your heart is so heavy. It's times like this that I knew Jesus had to be carrying me. You are not alone. Jesus is there to carry you too.

Sometimes, circumstances are just much bigger than you, particularly when God puts you in a situation where you know you can't "fix" it. As parents, that's what we do. We "fix" it. Having the inability to fix this was no accident either. You have to turn it over and put it in God's hands. This was a true test of faith for me and it will be for you as well, but remember, this is only a test. Day after day led to month after month and in my case led to year after year. I held on for dear life to His garment. I now encourage you to hold on to His garment and DON'T LET GO! Besides, He won't.

Introduction

Youth incarceration is increasing at alarming rates. It crosses all ages, races, gender and class groups. More than 2 million kids are arrested each year in the United States with a staggering estimate of 5 billion dollars annually being spent on juvenile courts. This is a HUGE for-profit industry. Nonetheless, if decisions in our communities are being made to invest in building the new jails and prisons, this means that the goal is to house them. Essentially, the new jails and prisons are being built for your kids and mine with a shift leaning disproportionally towards black males.

I am writing this book because I am a single mom who had to quickly learn about the judicial system in effort to advocate on my son's behalf. It is my goal to share insight into my journey in effort to enlighten and educate you on elements of the justice system. It is my hope that it will provide you with the necessary tools so that you will have a knowledge base that may be helpful in your decision-making process on a proactive basis. In addition, I want to provide you with the encouragement that you will definitely need through this

Introduction

difficult time. If you feel the need to even read this book, know that I've been there. I do understand that pain that you feel, I have been there. I can tell you NOTHING about this experience will be easy. I will affectionately reference the word "son", a theme that will be utilized throughout this book, however, is not meant to be gender specific.

This experience will teach you just how strong you really are, learn more about the God you serve as He works on your behalf, and see how you can grow even stronger in the Lord. Please allow me to walk with you through this journey. I quickly learned the first and last thing you should do is pray. I can tell you this experience hurt me to the core. I personally would not wish my experience on my worst enemy. I know it changed me, but it also taught me how much I truly loved my son and that God loved Him even more. God delivered my son and I am often asked, "How did I do it? How did you make it through because your son is doing so well now?" The answer is: I didn't do it, God did.

I'm sharing my story with you because my experience wasn't meant for me to go through and to keep to myself. In the midst of it all, I believed my story was meant to be shared and to be a blessing to others. The blessing wasn't just supposed to be for me and my family, but a testimony of

Introduction

encouragement to all who are going through similar situations. I never knew exactly how the story would end, but I didn't have to know. All I did know was that God was to get the glory in the end.

Introduction

Chapter 1

I Need Help!

I Need Help!

I Need Help!

My son did not have a father figure in his life other than my father who lived in another city. He talked to and poured knowledge into my son when he could from a distance. I was previously married to my son's father, but we separated and later divorced so he grew up without his Dad in his life. I didn't have a college degree at the time and didn't have any job training, but I didn't want my kids to grow up seeing their mother miserable in an unhappy household just for the sake of the kids. My ex-husband basically disappeared after the divorce, so we never knew where his father lived most of the time. I did the best I could and took the approach that all I needed was Jesus. I was not alone because He was going to help me, and He did. God knows the end to the beginning so for my journey, I will provide you with the same approach.

I am a single mom of three adult children. As we are all continuously evolving to better ourselves, ultimately my son ended up going off to college to become an engineer, my oldest daughter is a pharmacist, and my youngest daughter is currently off in college studying to become a psychiatrist. I am super proud of all of them and believe me, if God can do it for me, surely, He can do it for you. While going through the chaos, not when you've come out on the other side but while you are in the midst of it all, it was HARD. Nonetheless, I was thanking

I Need Help!

Him for the outcome even though I didn't know what it would look like. I encourage you to thank him for how the story ends. Start now. You have to trust Him completely, even with someone as precious as your children and yet even when you don't know what the end looks like. Start expressing the gratitude now for how your story ends. Keeping my end in mind, this is how my story unfolds.

My journey actually began in a war zone. It was not the warzone being fought domestically or abroad nor was it the war on crime being fought in the streets every day. Nonetheless, the biggest battle was being fought in my own home and it was spiritual warfare in the flesh. Things started to change as my son reached puberty. I had gone back to college and finished my undergraduate degree and now I was working a full-time job while working on my Masters. During this time, it was clear that I had a teenage son who was troubled. He appeared to be quiet and unhappy most of the time and I needed something greater than me to help me communicate with him. Things were CRAZY and unpredictable. At the age of 15, school would dismiss, and my son wasn't coming straight home. I didn't know where he was when he wasn't home. There was no communication, however, I knew he kept a female friend. I didn't know who his other friends were or if he had any other

I Need Help!

real friends for that matter and this was problematic for me. I didn't know any of them to call on if I were looking for him. What I did know for certain was that he was very full of promise meaning he was a very intellectual young man. You couldn't just have a regular conversation with him, he made you think. Just one deep conversation with him, you knew he was naturally smart, and he was challenging you mentally. You had to bring your A-game with him. The problem I was having was as many young men battle with, I knew he was going through many internal battles of self- discovery of his manhood. Through this really thick and tough exterior, I didn't think he knew where he fit in this world as a man because there wasn't anyone available to mentor him and show him what real men do or what defines a man.

As I felt things were escalating as my son increasingly became more and more disruptive in our home, one evening I made the call for the authorities to come and pick him up. It was literally the toughest thing I've ever had to do. They came to the house, lights flashing and ready to take a report. I stated my case and requested that they take him. Not knowing how this process worked, I requested that if they were going to use cuffs, not to do it in my house; I couldn't bear to see it. I felt so bad all I could do was cry but only after he left. I wept for

I Need Help!

my son. He was genuinely a good kid with a huge heart; however, his behavior was not reflective of the son that I had raised. I just didn't recognize his heart. I am sure if you are reading this book, you know what I mean. For me to make that call, it was totally against everything I believed but I didn't know what else to do. It was devastating for both of us I'm sure, but I just wanted things to get better and they weren't. We were both suffering in our own way, yet the common denominator was this was indeed a cry for help.

The authorities took him to the juvenile detention center (a.k.a. juvey) and later called for me to come and pick him up. They said that they had had problems with overcrowding. I was confused because I needed help but at the same time, I understood. From their perspective, a mom who didn't want her son to stay in the home for the night did not place high on their list. Honestly, part of me didn't want to pick him up because I felt he was safer there than on the streets and besides, at least I would know where he was. I picked him up, but I still felt helpless. I began to think well what if I had a man in my life to provide me insight to raising a young man. Nonetheless, personal relationships with men were not a high priority for me because I was busy raising 3 children. There were times when I thought I found someone to help me, that was frustrating

I Need Help!

because they wanted something more from me, so that wasn't an option. I tried to reach out to my mega-church for assistance. I took him to see the Youth Pastor twice, but nothing became of that. There wasn't a plan in place for troubled youth at the time and although they may have something now, they didn't then, so that wasn't a real option for help. So now, I found myself calling juvey to keep him there for a while and that was not an option either. It wasn't looking good for me. I needed some help fast, but I could not find any real help. So, I turned to God and started asking Him. Well, lesson learned, be careful what you ask for. He heard my every word. When God showed up, He came through in a way that I wasn't expecting or honestly as a mother, I personally would not have chosen at all due to the pain inflicted. (I guess that's why He is the Father.) It was my worst-case scenario.

One evening my son didn't come home and it was getting late. I started making my calls looking for him everywhere I could think to look. Later that night, I found out that my son had been arrested and taken to juvey. This time, they were not going to release him. I admit I was scared. All the questions in my mind started flowing back to back:

- ❖ Now What?
- ❖ What happened?

I Need Help!

- ❖ What did he do? I hope it's not too serious.
- ❖ What do we do now?
- ❖ Who can help us?
- ❖ Lord, why me? Why do I have to go through this?
- ❖ What did I do wrong?
- ❖ Did I do anything wrong?
- ❖ What didn't I do?
- ❖ What am I supposed to do?
- ❖ Who do I tell?
- ❖ Can I tell anyone?
- ❖ Where is God? ... Now when I made it to this question …and you will get to this question, this is when I knew God had stepped in. Just knowing that God had gotten involved, I immediately went into prayer.

I Need Help!

Daddy,

Please bless my child. Help him to see through all the enemies' distractions. Help him to know that you are still in control and that he's your child. Jesus keep him covered and protected by your blood now and forevermore. I ask that you bless him with wisdom and strength. For with wisdom he will clearly discern right from wrong and with strength to be able to actually do the right thing.

I know there is spiritual warfare going on with my child. But Lord, I believe you are more powerful than any force on this earth. All I have to do is call on your name. Well, Jesus, I need you. I can't do this by myself. My son needs you, whether he knows it or not. There is good in everybody. There's a lot of good in him but he's making bad choices. Please, please Lord, save my child. Save him before he makes choices that will put him in a situation neither he nor I can get him out of. I'm being proactive Lord because I'm coming to you. I may have tried talking to him and other people when I should have brought him to you first. Forgive me for that but I'm coming now as humble as I know how. Take him and walk with him. Holy Spirit, take him and talk to him. Daddy, you made him, change his heart and change his mind. Remove all that is not of you and replace it with everything that is of you. Have your way so that his purpose may be served, and your name may be glorified in the end.

In Jesus name I pray. Amen.

I Need Help!

I had been praying through this entire process but when God stepped in, I admit, I didn't like the answer. Incarceration!!! What??? That's not what I asked for. Lord, there must have been a mistake. I asked for your help but not that kind of help. In my opinion, that was really my worst-case scenario!

My mind started messing with me because I couldn't help but keep coming back to what if I had a man in my life on a consistent basis to guide him. I knew he needed a male role model in his life, but I didn't have a solution. I felt stuck. I thought he was going through puberty maybe, rites of passage rituals and everything else because I'm not a man, but I assumed he was just trying to find and identify his manhood. You can call it what you want but whatever it was, I couldn't reach him. As a woman trying to raise this young man of mine, there was no way for me to know all the questions he may have had:

- My body looks like a man but am I a man?
- What defines a man?
- Do I fit the qualifications?
- How do I find out what a man really is?
- Who will teach me?
- I have all this extra energy, what do I do with it?

I Need Help!

- ❖ Where is the challenge to see if I am a man?
- ❖ I think I'm ready for the test so how can I test myself?

As a mother, you have no real idea what goes on in the mind of your son. Nonetheless, one thing that you know for sure is that the energy needs to be channeled in the right direction or nothing good will come out of it. God allowed me to be in this situation, so I had to step back and get out of God's way.

It hurt to see us going down this road but at the same time, I also knew something had to be done. I didn't like the route we were taking because I personally thought it was embarrassing even though no one else knew what was going on but my other children. I still felt a sense of shame, but I had to put my pride and ego to the side because this wasn't about me. I felt like I had good kids and we all were doing well when you view us from the outside looking in. As a family unit, the perception was that we reflected promise. This was the expectation. Nonetheless, my son was more important than how we were being perceived. All that positive image stuff went out the window and I didn't care about the perception anymore because one of us was suffering. As a mother, I just felt if one of us wasn't okay, none of us were okay. I knew I had to trust God and that God knew what was best. My actions and decisions weren't working so I had to turn it over and let go

I Need Help!

and let God. After I fought the big fight of trying to control my situation with my son which clearly was a losing battle, I had to release him to his Daddy, his heavenly father. He kept telling me, "Lisa, give him to me. Lisa! Lisa!!!! Give him to me." I still fought tooth and nail, but I had to trust Him. I finally gave in and released my son over to God; we had a long talk. Actually, it was more I stopped doing all the talking and started listening. Man, what a difference. I decided to let go and stop trying to be God and let God be God. It took 100% trust.

The Miranda Warning

The Miranda Warning

Chapter 2

The Miranda Warning

The Miranda Warning

The Miranda Warning

At some point during the arrest, the police should verbally state the Miranda Warning. The Miranda Warning is a group of rights that should be read to you at the time of your arrest. These are your constitutional rights provided to every U.S. citizen. In my opinion, unfortunately, many citizens fail to use them particularly if you are young and really don't know any better. It is important that we educate our children so that they know that they should be provided with this Miranda Warning, what it means to them and that there are things they can say that will benefit them later.

Miranda Warning:

- ❖ You have the right to remain silent.
- ❖ Anything you say can and will be used against you in the court of law.
- ❖ You have the right to an attorney.
- ❖ If you cannot afford an attorney, one will be provided for you.
- ❖ Do you understand the rights that I have just read to you? With this in mind, do you wish to speak to me?

Law enforcement are people just like you and me. It just so happens that it is their job to enforce the law. Some do it better than others. Some are nice, knowledgeable and are genuinely good people. Many of us may have one or two in our families. They do their job and do their job well to provide the protection to the community that we so desperately need. I applaud them. However, there are still bad cops that we cannot deny exist that may be working at the same station. At times when no one is looking, they break the laws themselves. They are allowed to be criminals and utilize the law to escape persecution. The criminal justice system is so dysfunctional starting with the police departments.

I had the arresting officers in my son's case to show up at the courtroom to speak on behalf of the prosecuting attorney's office. It made me feel a certain kind of way because their goal was to ensure they had a solid case against my son. They made time out of their schedule to make sure he would not go free. I felt like, "Really?" Whether your son encounters a good cop or a bad cop, at the time of an arrest, he should be read the Miranda Warning.

1: You Have The Right To Remain Silent!!!!

Do NOT confess to ANYTHING particularly at the scene.

The Miranda Warning

Do NOT speak with ANY law enforcement or allow yourself to be intimidated into speaking to officials without legal representation. If you are cohoarsed into saying anything, the only relevant word you should speak is: L-a-w-y-e-r.

The first right that is recited to you by law enforcement is the RIGHT to remain silent! This means that, yes; you do have the right not to speak with law enforcement. If it is clear that there is a crime committed, in any state within the United States of America, one of your human rights is that: You are innocent until "proven" guilty. This means if you commit a crime or there is criminal activity occurring, the police will be called. If you have anything to do with the crime, it is easy to be scared and intimidated by so many officers crowding around you with all the bright shining lights asking you all these questions. They may (not) have their notepads out documenting your every word to any question they see fit to ask you at the time. You are positioned all alone and you have been raised to respect authorities, be honest and truthful. This is the way my son was raised very much like millions of other young men in this country so when asked by authorities what did he do wrong, naturally he was truthful the way I taught him to be. I was actually proud of the character and integrity he displayed at that time. I later learned that it would have been in his best interest

The Miranda Warning

to wait to speak with his attorney first. I didn't know any better and therefore, I had not educated him on his rights that in that instance, it would have been more beneficial to inform the officers that he would just like to speak with his attorney.

Everything you say at the scene can critically hurt you later in court. So the best approach is to determine early what will work to your advantage. If you suspect that a crime has been committed, you will definitely need representation and your right to remain silent comes into play. Why make it easy for law enforcement to convict you? Think things through at the scene. It is as simple as if you think for an instant that you may need an attorney, remain silent; the attorney can speak on your behalf. Admission of guilt at the time of the scene is a sure-fire way that potentially may cause you to go to jail or prison all because you were scared at that moment.

If you choose to remain silent, you need to inform the officers with your words verbally where everyone can hear, that you "choose" to remain silent. It goes something like this: "Sir, I choose to remain silent" and/or alternate with "I would like to speak with my attorney Sir" to every question that is asked of you. You have not admitted to anything or denied anything. You are just requesting to speak with your attorney and there is nothing wrong with that. You do not have to tell anyone

The Miranda Warning

anything, however, the only thing that you must provide is your correct name as this varies per state. If they request your I.D., provide that as well. Now, keep in mind, at this point the questioning is supposed to stop but that doesn't mean that it will. At the time of an arrest, adrenaline is high, and the real question is: Do you have the ability to remain silent? Keep in mind, if they can get you to answer one question, that will lead to you answering another question to justify the one response and it's a downward slope. This interrogation can continue on site or at the police station by asking you an additional 1 to 100 questions which leads to your second right.

2: "Anything" You Say Can And Will Be Used Against You.

Any officer doing his job well will try to get a confession at the time of the scene. They can utilize the chaos from the scene to their advantage so any verbal information will be utilized to get a conviction. Your son needs to know that he should wait to contact his public defender or attorney immediately and do not discuss his case with anyone but his attorney. Authorities are aware that most people are scared and afraid of the unknown at the time of the arrest. They know that this is the best time to get pertinent information upfront when emotions are high, and

The Miranda Warning

youth are feeling vulnerable? It is in the best interest of the police to utilize the scene to their advantage. Obtaining information on the scene is time-sensitive and may be critical to their case particularly for youth. Sometimes the police will get all of their information first before making an arrest based on the information they have received. They can gather the information from everyone and then they decide whom to arrest. This can occur if there is more than one person of interest, evidence is unclear, and no one has spoken to the other or everyone gets arrested anyway. Either way, if police are called to a crime scene, they are called there for a reason and someone is going to get questioned.

Some believe that in a worst-case scenario, if you are arrested at the scene and you know that you did not commit the crime and you would not confess to the really nice officer who wanted to have a nice conversation with you at the scene, there may be consequences waiting at the station. Just in case your son is placed in this unfortunate situation, he needs to be prepared for a lengthy interrogation at the police station by police who are trained in interrogation. Again, he needs to stay strong and wait for his attorney. The more he keeps silent; the better case he will have for his defense. His job is to place himself in the best position so that he won't have to stay in jail or return. When he does meet with his attorney, the first thing they are going to want is to determine how much damage to the case has already been done. If the client talked, it only hurts the case and they are digging you out of a mess. The less information provided to authorities, gives your council something to work with on your behalf.

3: You Have A Right To An Attorney...

When your rights are being read to you, law enforcement will tell you, "You have a right to an attorney..." so requesting to speak with this individual is perfectly legal and within your rights. This means that you shouldn't feel out of line when letting the officer know that you would like to speak with your lawyer prior to speaking with him. Our nature is to be respectful and wanting to comply with an officer who is asking us questions. However, in this situation, we have rights that we need to utilize for our best interest respectfully.

In waiting to speak with your attorney, this does several things:

- ❖ It puts the power back in your hands in the long run.
- ❖ It prohibits evidence of a verbal and/or signed confession.

The Miranda Warning

- ❖ It prohibits evidence of admission to the crime that may (not) be found at the scene to be connected with you.

- ❖ It makes the authorities have to work for the information to try to put the pieces together opposed to you just hand delivering them a case against you.

Some people confess upfront right on the scene, and it makes law enforcement job very easy but ... it deeply hurts you later. We need to teach our children to wait to speak with an attorney who can work on their behalf. By speaking with the authorities, prior to speaking with your attorney, you are digging a hole for your attorney. The first couple of hours at the arrest scene are critical to everything that follows and sets the tone for everything else to come. Teach them to remember: REQUEST TO SPEAK TO AN ATTORNEY!

4: "And If You Don't Have An Attorney, One Will Be Assigned To You".

If you do not have the funds to hire a private attorney, an attorney will be assigned to represent your case by the court at no charge to you. These attorneys are called public defenders who are essentially attorneys hired to defend the public at no cost to you. Like many attorneys, they will have multiple cases but rest assured, they are swamped. The courts are full of cases that come through the court system on a daily basis so your case can very well get thrown in the pile with the rest if you don't stay on top of it.

Throughout my entire process, we had several public defenders. It was our first public defender that I learned the most from due to his lack of knowledge. He was not prepared, and I don't believe he even looked at our case until right before we walked into court. I had to bring him up to speed on information that I felt he should have already known prior to the hearing. This taught me I needed to take the responsibility to ensure that they remembered my son's case.

Be sure to keep in constant communication with your attorney to ensure that they are knowledgeable who your son is and the status of the case at all times. This will help when a hearing is called; they won't have to do as much research to familiarize themselves with your case on the spare of the moment because your case is in the forethought of their mind. I asked questions like:

- ❖ Have you heard any news?
- ❖ What is the status of my case?

- Have you been to see him?
- How does he look?
- How is he holding up?
- Did he say anything about his case?
- What do I need to know?
- Is there anything I can do to help?
- What are your plans to handle this?

The key is to stay in touch with your attorney. You want to ensure that your case won't be treated like a number. This relationship is critical to your case because this individual is the voice of your son in that courtroom, so they need to understand that they are fighting for someone who is worth the fight. Who can convey that message better than you?

5: Do You Understand The Rights That I Have Just Read To You? With These Rights In Mind, Do You Wish To Speak To Me?

Any typical young man will answer a question when asked by authorities in any given situation, however, in this situation where a law may be broken, if your son decides to speak with the officers by providing information after the rights have been read, they have in essence just waived the Miranda

The Miranda Warning

warning/rights. This means they previously had court authorized rights that they have now waived and everything that they say can and will be used against them. I don't have to be an attorney to say this is not advised.

This question acknowledges that there is a mutual agreement to which you understand all that the officer has informed you regarding your rights. If your son responds, "yes" to this question, then anything following this response is fair game.

I can give you a prime example of using the law to your advantage. We currently have a politician serving in public office who proudly confesses that he doesn't pay taxes because he is smart. He elaborated by stating that he follows the "law" to get out of paying his (fair share) of taxes. It saves him MILLIONS of dollars by following the law. The same principle applies here. At the scene or the time of the arrest, the police gives you the Miranda Warning advising you of your rights. They inform you that you have a right to an attorney and that everything you say can and will be held against you. The question is, "Why aren't we using those rights?" This is what we need to teach our children. This is the same as the billionaire knowing the law but not applying it to his circumstance and paying millions of dollars that he claims he didn't have to pay.

The Miranda Warning

It is the law so he's using it. The question is: Why aren't we??? All of our children and adults for that matter, should be yelling, "I want to speak with my lawyer!!!" There shouldn't be any Dateline television shows with scenes from investigation rooms with our young men sitting alone with police officers providing confessions without legal representation. What it comes down to is that you have rights ... USE them. We have to change the mindset.

Questions For The Authorities

Questions For The Authorities

Chapter 3
Questions For The Authorities

Questions For The Authorities

Questions For The Authorities

Soon after the arrest and your son has been advised of his Miranda Warning/Rights, he is taken into custody. He will be fingerprinted and placed in holding. An initial court hearing will generally be set very soon after the offense has been committed so you must act fast to find out as much information as you can. If you missed the initial hearing, then you need to know when the next court date will be and what may have transpired but you want to obtain as much information as you can from the authorities when you speak with them on the phone. Some of the following questions are instrumental when speaking with the authorities. Here are a few questions that I asked:

What are the charges?

You want to know this for you to conduct your own research to determine the seriousness of the crime. Find out if the offense is a misdemeanor or felony. (I will discuss the difference and significance in detail later). You will also want to know which level? A, B, C...? It is equally important.

Has the initial court hearing been set?

Since the initial court hearing will generally be set very soon after the offense has been committed, you must act fast

Questions For The Authorities

to ask as many questions to the authorities as you need to in effort to sooth your mind and bring you some peace. In addition, if there is something you do not understand, you can always ask for clarification. If you still do not understand the response, you ask again and again until you are comfortable with what you are hearing, and you comprehend the response. You ask questions to them simply because that is what they are there for; to work on your behalf and the behalf of your son.

At the initial court hearing, it will be determined who will represent your son whether it will be a public or private attorney. If you already have a private attorney in mind, you will want to bring him up to speed prior to the hearing so that he can attend. The judge will reschedule the hearing for your son to plead guilty or not guilty to the charges.

In many cases, do not be surprised if additional minor charges are added on to the most prominent crime. For instance, if the crime is assault, resisting arrest or battery may be added. The more charges added, the likelihood that at least one will stick in the end to warrant a sentence. Rarely is an arrest solely for only one offense. Once you find out what the offenses are, now it is time to find out what you're up against as it relates to the maximum time the offense has for sentencing so that you can know what the worst-case scenario may be.

Questions For The Authorities

This is relevant because time issued under state law is different from time issued under federal law.

Once your son has been taken into custody and the initial hearing is set, the judge will ask if he has an attorney to represent him. If you don't have the money to hire a law firm to represent you, a public defender will be assigned by the courts.

Who is the Public Defender assigned to my case?

A Public Defender is a lawyer employed at no cost to the defendant which is a pro- bono attorney assigned to the courts in a criminal trial to represent a defendant who is unable to afford legal assistance. You will want to know specifically who the attorney is assigned to your son's case. The public defender may (not) be assigned until the day of the initial hearing or soon after. When the public defenders are assigned to a particular case, at some point, they have the option to go and visit your son to find out the details as to what really happened. The details will be critical to the charges applied not limited to but to include if there was a confession? You need to know because if there was a confession, that eliminates innocent until proven guilty unless there is proof of a forced confession.

Questions For The Authorities

If your son is kept at the juvenile detention center prior to the hearing, the Public Defender can meet with his client literally right before going into the court room. At the next hearing, you may have a different Public Defender assigned to your son's case. In our case, it was clear that with each new Public Defender, he did not have a very thorough knowledge of my son's case. He had some understanding but at a very high level. One appeared to be very robotic and this was of great concern to me. I later learned that they typically have so many cases that it is nearly impossible for them to know all of their cases thoroughly. It quickly became clear that it was my responsibility to make sure that my Public Defender needed to be able to distinguish my son's case from all of his other cases. I could not afford to allow my son to be slipped through the cracks.

You want to know that the person representing you is working on your behalf so it would be beneficial to ask several questions to ensure that they are working "with" you. The goal in asking all of these questions is to allow your representative to "connect" with you. They need to know that this child is not to be viewed as just another case. They need to understand that he has a mother that cares, loves their child, cares about what happens to them and to understand that you want to be

Questions For The Authorities

involved in this process. When they can tell you that they have a child and they would ask the same questions or be just as concerned, you know that you have connected with them. When this case comes up in court, you want them to make the mental connection with you which means they will in turn hopefully care just a little bit more than the norm.

What is the process?

Simply because I was totally oblivious to the system, I felt like a deer in headlights. LOST! So I had many questions. I needed to know what I was facing and regardless of how big the mountain, I was going to climb it because I refused to allow my son to go through this by himself. In effort for me to stay one step ahead, I needed to know what was coming down the pipeline. What can happen, the possibilities, the odds, the judges if they were partial or impartial, I ask questions until I had peace of mind.

What are my next steps?

If there is anything you can do to help in this process, you will want to know the efforts you can make in advance so that you can be prepared. They know more than you so this is the question I would get in the habit of asking when you don't know what is going to happen next. For instance, I was told the more family members that attended the court hearings to show support could help the judge see that there are people who care for the well-being of your son other than one parent. I had no family members in my city so I couldn't do anything about this; however, this is an example of something that could work in the favor of your son. Each case is different, and you never know what the judge is thinking. It is just good to know certain information so that you can plan in advance. In addition, having the knowledge of what may potentially be on the horizon can also help soften the blow where you are not caught off guard in extreme circumstances.

God Needed To Get His Attention.

As a parent, you know better than anyone that things needed to change for the better and it was something that only God can do. So, you prayed and you prayed and guess what? God heard each and every word of your prayers. You are hurting right now but know that God also knows your pain. He wants you to trust him. If you're going through this situation, trust in God should not be optional. We start by letting go through relinquishing what we thought was our control and releasing the wheel. Turn your son over. Believe me, I get it.

Questions For The Authorities

The confusing and disturbing part about this is you're questioning the method that God is choosing to utilize:

- ❖ Lord, does he have to go to jail?
- ❖ Is all this necessary?
- ❖ That's my son! He doesn't know anything about judicial systems! Do you have to get his attention this way???
- ❖ Why this method?
- ❖ Couldn't you use another route?
- ❖ What will people say?
- ❖ What will people think?

I want to emphasize; Let go and Let God. You have to remember, that was God's son before he was yours. Your son is on loan to you. God is allowing you to raise, nurture and take care of His son but don't get it twisted, that's really His baby, therefore, don't ever underestimate His love for him. God has been watching all this mayhem that's been going on too. He is the Daddy! So, how long did you expect Him as a father, to sit by and allow the mayhem to go on? He already knew when your son would start clowning and He knows when he will stop, grow up and mature and move on to the next phase in his life. None of this came as a surprise to Him. The hardest and the easiest part is to trust Him.

Questions For The Authorities

What you need to do is to continue praying but the difference is, now you know that God has His hands on your son. God chose to use this approach to gain your sons attention and you have to trust in what God is doing even when it doesn't make sense to you.

> *5 Trust in the Lord with all your heart,*
>
> *And lean not on your own understanding;*
>
> *6 In all your ways acknowledge Him,*
>
> *And He shall direct your paths*
>
> *Proverbs 3:5-6*

In knowing that God has His hands on your son, despite the circumstances, think about it, what better place can he be?

It's a reminder that in times like this, that the primary focus should not be about our sons. The kids are going to do what they do whether we like it or not. Some will listen and get it the first time while others will make a different decision. As some of us see our sons go through a difficult puberty stage, we know in the pit of our stomach that our child is headed in the wrong direction, and yet we don't know how it's going to end up. With this feeling of something bad on the horizon, I NEED to encourage you to understand that the focus should be

Questions For The Authorities

consistently on God. Keep your eyes on God. Depending on how rough our storm gets, we tend to lose sight of who's really running the show, who's calling the shots and who's allowing things to happen to and around us.

We sometimes feel that we're praying and that our prayers are going unanswered. If they are going unanswered, THANK Him because He knows what's best and that means He's working in the background. This is where your trust plays a pivotal role. He could also be answering your prayers but going about it in a way other than what you may feel is the best solution or what you had envisioned for your child. Realistically, who plans for their child to be arrested? Keep in mind, God is the author and He knows what He is doing. We sometimes feel God had abandoned us right when we need him the most because we can't hear Him or maybe because He's silent. If your child has been arrested, trust me, God is not silent. Sometimes, maybe He just wants to know if you'll still trust Him. How strong is your faith? And how do we get through this type of pain? This is foreign territory. And when it gets really bad, you find yourself asking, "Where is God and will this pain ever let up? The answer is "Yes". Why? Because trouble don't last always.

This TOO shall pass.

Questions For The Authorities

Life isn't just a journey ...it's also a test along the way. He hears you. When you've reached your limit, then God can begin to do His work. We sometimes tend to hold on and want to control things, but certain situations can be totally out of our control. This is a very uncomfortable place for most. He has not forgotten you.

Overcrowding

There was an occasion where the authorities called and requested that I come and pick up my son due to overflow. The juvenile detention center was full to capacity and they were releasing some of the youth of promise that were not considered a "high risk". However, he was required to return at a later date for the initial court hearing in a week. In the meantime, he was provided the name of a Public Defender, the name of a Probation Officer that he had to touch base with prior to the court date and eventually, an ankle bracelet. My son contacted the Probation Officer just to check in who was assigned to his case.

When we arrived to pick him up, we went through a different entrance. It appeared to have a very jail-like atmosphere. The authorities at intake went through my purse and we went through metal detectors. I told them why we were there, and we were led to a room. Walking through each corridor was a thick metal door that slammed hard and locked behind us. It was very intimidating to say the least. It felt like I was living a jail scene on TV. I don't consider myself bougie, but I honestly felt bougie being there.

Before they would release him to me, there was a process I had to go through. There was an intake coordinator in a law enforcement uniform asking me to answer detailed questions not just about my son, but about each member of our family. At that moment, I felt like we were providing the personal information for the criminal justice system application. I also began to feel like they wanted this information because my son was getting close to the age of 18. It felt like we were completing the formal application for entrance into the criminal justice system. It felt like as his family, we were being signed up too. There was no turning back at this point. Make no mistake; we were all in this together. They wanted to know information as if they were the FBI; they wanted social security numbers, all the addresses of where I've ever lived, schools that each family member has ever attended, the grades my children were in, closest relatives, emergency contacts, everything that connects us together as a unit. Like all applications, I had to sign that all the information I provided was true. I had no idea what lie ahead of us, but this was not a good feeling at all. Everything about this experience felt bad.

Time To Regroup - Everything Happens For A Reason

Your son may have made a mistake, but his truth may be that he has probably made several mistakes before and this time, he just got caught. There are many good kids who go through phases in their life where they push the envelope, and some end up in serious trouble; trouble with drugs or ultimately trouble with the law. It is my firm belief that all kids are good, they have a good heart and they are still that precious child that you raised and raised well. The memories are real and not to be forgotten. Then at some point, we blinked. Life stepped in and their bodies change physically. They are affected by the environmental, social, mental, psychological and spiritual influences around them. They grew up.

The kids today are a new breed. You rarely hear, "Yes ma'am" and "No Sir" total opposite of when our parents were kids. They have social media that displays life in real time on the other side of the world. The media has been a contributing influence in and framing their mindset. Therefore, we find ourselves with kids who watch more violence on TV that is

Questions For The Authorities

designed to be as real as real gets and we are there to catch the brunt of it all wondering, "Who are you and what did you do with my kid? This isn't the way I raised you." But when you see your son heading down the wrong path, you know deep in your spirit that things cannot continue this way.

Something has to give. God is not going to sit back and allow this behavior because he disciplines those he loves. As you watch this terrible movie being played out, you know in your spirit that something has to give. You just don't know the what or how, but the thought scares you because you know it is going to involve God in order for real change to come. You know that's HIS son acting a fool and He's not just going to sit by and watch the show. Well, something will give and if you are reading this book, God has stepped in. Everything happens for a reason.

The thing that you have to remember and find great comfort in is knowing that God wrote the script. This means He already knows the outcome. As many versions of the story that we play in our mind, God knows how the story ends. Our decisions may dictate which plot gets played out and it may increase or decrease the length of the story but just as long as the outcome is still the same, that is where we can find the peace. But the cool part about it is, He uses our bad decisions that may have increased the length of the story as lessons that we can pull from later. If we don't learn the first, second or third time, He loves us enough to be patient with us until we do get it. Every element of our story line is significant, and it all plays a role in the big picture. This is why when you see a child, what you are really looking at is a big ball of potential. Never underestimate what God can do with a child. All they have is life ahead of them and lots of it. The thing is to just keep on living and don't give up on them. You were once that child and God's hands are still on you. The same is true for your son. His journey just may be a little different from yours and that's okay but just know that God is still working on Him. God knows the timing that things should take place, the order and the magnitude of the brunt. He knows how much pain you can handle and how big the blessing. Everybody is different and no one will have the same journey, but we have to just trust that He is God and allow Him to be just that… GOD. So, take your hands off the wheel.

Questions For The Authorities

Let The Court Hearings Begin

Chapter 4

Let The Court Hearings Begin

Let The Court Hearings Begin

Let The Court Hearings Begin

In the courtroom, the judge will read the offenses giving your son an opportunity to plead guilty or not guilty. I would highly recommend that your son's legal representative suggest to your son to plead "not guilty" allowing him time to familiarize himself with the case. That would only make sense. After hearing the not guilty plea, the judge will then reschedule for a "continuance" to return at a later date.

It would be to your advantage to expect that there will be several continuances. With each continuance, my son had to stay in the Juvenile Detention Center a.k.a. "juvey". Hearings were scheduled on a monthly basis or every other month contingent on the availability in the judge's schedule. Nonetheless, I was shocked and surprised to find that after the court date had been scheduled, it was set to accommodate the next available magistrate or judge. This meant that not only are you possibly rotating attorneys but also judges as well. Since these kids are just a number to the system, when we would return to court, a different judge would be working the bench. The problems I felt with this was (1) this judge was not knowledgeable of all that had already taken place, (2) you are not familiar with this new judge or their temperament and (3) this judge knows nothing of what may have happened in the

Let The Court Hearings Begin

past court hearings that was not documented. It is the equivalent to going to court for child support and developing a rapport with the judge on the bench who has heard details of your case even though much of it isn't in the notes. You then return to court time after time to find a new judge sitting on the bench and having to start all over from scratch. There was no real way to prepare for every hearing because you never knew what or who to expect. It was like playing a numbers game. Every once in a while, you would get the judge you were hoping for that you knew was familiar with your case and may have cared a little more than others. My son's future was in the hands of a complete stranger who was reading cliff notes with no knowledge of all the had taken place prior to that day. Every hearing was a whole new ball game with my sons life on the line. We never knew what to expect as each magistrate brought their own temperament and they varied.

In the courtroom, it felt like this was a job that had gotten old to everyone there. It was a very unemotional, detached and robotic atmosphere. Each case lasted no more than 15 minutes and they were rotating those black (young) men through that system like clockwork. It felt like this is what's happening all day, every day to people of color not just in this courtroom, but in most courtrooms across this country.

Let The Court Hearings Begin

In my observation, the waiting rooms were filled to capacity primarily with black women and children, however, in the courtroom, everyone there was white with the exception of the bailiffs who wore guns and the defendants in cuffs. Everyone else was white. All that I had heard about the broken criminal justice system was staring me in the face. I quickly realized that this was a reflection of our criminal justice system in America. Our young black men were being treated like cattle, each given a number as an identity, all shackled to one another as they were treated and transported like modern day slaves. Now let your brain marinate on that for a minute.

As I sat there in court, I couldn't help but realize that I was feeling so many emotions all at once and they were all negative. I had feelings of anger, disappointment, rage and my heart was simply broken. I have had many thoughts since then that prompted me to pay more attention to the criminal justice system in America and I sarcastically say, the beautiful.

Released With An Ankle Bracelet

Based on the severity of the offence, your son can be released for probation and sent home which is called In-home Detention. This means they will release him into your care provided that he signs up for an ankle monitor service.

Let The Court Hearings Begin

Probation is not only designed to be an inconvenience to him, but it will also be an inconvenience on the family if he's living at home.

A company has a contractual agreement that provides the ankle monitors. This is usually done by attaching a wireless ankle bracelet to the ankle that communicates with a system that is placed inside the home. The ankle bracelet must be worn at all times even in the shower. The system is there to serve as a tracking database for the authorities to basically track his whereabouts. The authorities will monitor his every move closely. If the courts indicate that he cannot go outside of a 1000 sq. ft. radius, then 1000 sq. ft. it will be. If going outside on the front porch or walking in the backyard extended further than the 1000 sq. ft. allotment, then the system will beep to notify authorities that he is out of range. They may or may not choose to follow-up, however, know that if the system beeps, it is being logged.

Now, if the beeping has occurred once or maybe too many times for the authorities, or if your son is not where he's supposed to be, at their discretion, they can find him in violation. If he violates probation, then the in-home detention is discontinued, and he is returned back to confinement.

Let The Court Hearings Begin

In our situation, the authorities came into our home to set up the system upon my son's release. They placed a box in a centralized location in our home and my son was instructed as to how far away from the box he could go. After a while, the ankle bracelet is designed to become annoying and with the limitations being so strict, it was all annoying like someone else was living in the house with us watching our every move. Nonetheless, I was just glad he was home, so we made it work. It wasn't going to be that easy though. There was a price for him to pay for being home even with the ankle bracelet. He still had to report to his probation officer on a regular basis and call him at certain times.

He could go to work or class as long as his probation officer knew in advance of all of his whereabouts so that the buzzer would not be going off needlessly. His school conveniently housed a probation officer onsite within the school for all of the young (black) men who were also on probation throughout the school year. Nonetheless, his time away from the house was very limited and with restrictions. In addition, because he was still a ward of the state, although he was home, he still wasn't free. The most difficult part of it was that at any given moment, day or night, whenever authorities saw fit, they could come by our home and check on him. I

Let The Court Hearings Begin

didn't mind during the day when I was at work and he would be home but when they started coming at 3:00 in the morning, I still was raising his 7-year old little sister. She didn't need that. And if they wanted to, they could walk around our home looking for what, I still do not know. I believe it was to see if there was anything laying around that shouldn't be in the home while he's there on probation such as alcohol. They fiddled with his ankle bracelet for him to make it tighter on his ankle.

Who would want some random officers to come to your home to inconvenience the family in the middle of the night disturbing the peace just to what it felt like agitate your son? I felt violated. If the beeper isn't going off, I felt it was very inconsiderate to the family. This was one of the worst rules in my opinion and I still don't understand it.

Nonetheless, after a while, time passed and after stepping too far away from the box too many times, there were too many beeps, they considered it a violation and he had to go back to juvey and because he was not a violent offender and no real threat to himself or society, he was allowed to come back home.

Anger

Anger

Chapter 5

Anger

Anger

Anger

You may visually witness in the truest form an emotion called anger. It may be through outburst, swelling up in the chest or what is spoken out of anger verbally but believe me, when it shows its ugly face, you will recognize it. It will not look like your son at all, but you will see the demon inside. This demon is there because of all that he has gone through in his life that you don't know about. You don't know what he's had to experience or see happen to other people.

He has been living in hell and therefore exposed to evil and he may have had to become evil in a sense just to survive. So it's possible, an evil nature may have followed him home. Do not be alarmed. With time, when evil meets the purest form of love a.k.a. God, evil has to flee. There is no match. There is no competition. You may have heard the saying, Love always wins." Love will win in the end. For him, be strong and show it.

He's still your son, he's just been through some things, but he will be fine. Think about it. For instance, if you relocated to another state for a job, it will take you time to get accustomed to your new environment. It's the same principle; it took him time to adjust to the environment of which he's had to live, and it wasn't all flowers and roses, but he had to adjust. Now that he's home, it's going to take him time to readjust to being

Anger

home. Give him that time with expectations to help with the adjustment process. Your rules are your rules but understand that the mind has to regroup. He has to learn an entirely new system. Another example is my oldest daughter once came home from college and wanted to label everything in the refrigerator like she had done with her roommates. I had to reiterate to her that she was "home" and you don't have to do that anymore. It has the same principle in that your son will need to re-acclimate back to his home environment.

Now, just naturally, you are going to ask the question, "Why is he SO angry?" More than likely, you have asked yourself this question more than once. The answer to this question, could me a multitude of things such as:

- ❖ The feelings of being lost and confused without direction
- ❖ The feelings of failing in school and/or life
- ❖ Being angry with you for things you may (not) know about
- ❖ Having the knowledge that you are constantly being targeted by police on a regular basis

This list could be endless particularly if you are a black man living in the United States. The reason your son is angry could

Anger

be a variety of things but only he can really tell you all the reasons why. As a woman, I can only speculate that it may have something to do with at least one of the three reasons below:

- ❖ His Father's Absence: No one to teach him how to be a man
- ❖ Feelings of Rejection
- ❖ Joblessness

You would have to be a (young) man living in today's world to really be able to articulate a response to that question for yourself. Each black man has their own story to tell of all the reasons to why. When you couple any of these alone with a multiple of other factors, it is enough to make anyone angry if they are constantly faced with these circumstances and endure feelings of helplessness. This can be a lot for a young man who wants to grow up and do something with his life.

Despite how angry your son may be, it's the love that has sustained you this far when you felt like you just couldn't take it anymore. You learned more about yourself through this experience than any self-help book that you could ever read. God showed you His face. You didn't know that you loved your son so much until you were faced with this situation and believe me; he learned how much you loved him too. It was that agape love, that unconditional love that no matter what he may have done wrong, he is still your son and that comes with benefits. Well guess what? Don't you see? That's how God feels about you. You are His daughter/son and that comes with benefits, blessings, abundance, the overflow, the more than enough. You are hanging in there because you love your son. You were there for him because you love him. You will get through this together because you love him …and by the way, you will get through. He's still the same kid you raised; he just has some debris on him that will come off with time. He's been through a storm and he's gotten a little dirty but underneath all that dirt is your son. It's a perfect trinity working at its best. When you take love (God) and you add eternal water (Jesus) to clean the dirt that is sticking to him from the outside and use internal water (the Holy Spirit) working from the inside out to clean the dirt that you are now seeing that is not the son you raised, the debris will have no choice but to fall off. Keep praying and watch what God does.

His Father's Absence: He was not there to Teach Him How to Be a Man

Many young men today are growing up in single family homes whereby the mother is raising the children. It's difficult to be a young man growing up in this environment without the biological father there to instruct him on how to become a man and demonstrate what a man looks like and the character that goes with manhood. He therefore finds himself questioning internally,

- ❖ "Am I really a man?
- ❖ I saw my body change but what defines a man?
- ❖ I may or may not have a job or something on the side to bring in some money but does that make me a man?
- ❖ What defines a man? There's no one to show or tell me so how do I really know?
- ❖ I think I am, or am I? My father isn't around when I need him? How will I figure this out?

These questions are normal but if there isn't a physical man of good character to help guide a young man, then they will seek out answers to their questions on their own. If they are introduced that a real man makes babies because the bible says be fruitful and multiply, well, babies will follow. They do this not knowing that be fruitful and multiply is to be interpreted as be productive with your time, with the God-given seeds that He gave you, use it and multiply your strengths in a productive way. All the time, there is resentment is building because the fulfillment of this void of defining what manhood really is in a way that they understand is not there when they

Anger

need it the most. How they chose to deal with these feeling of resentment vary.

All Little Boys Need Guidance and Direction from the Father

- Iyanla Vanzant

When a little boy doesn't have a father to show him the way, he can never be quite sure about the "manhood things" he needs to know. He's never quite sure about how strong is strong enough; how soft is too soft; or how much doing or giving is enough from a "man's point of view". He's never quite sure how to push forward or when to pull back. When a little boy doesn't have a father to guide him, he's not sure when to speak up or when to shut up. A little boy who does not or did not have a father is never quite sure what other men will think about what he has to say.

Some little boys grow up never feeling quite sure about the things their fathers did not or could not teach them. Sometimes they figure things out on their own, by and error. Still, they are not quite sure about themselves. They grieve silently in their hearts, which does not make them feel good about the man they are or are becoming. Many little boys grow up to be men who do not realize that they have a heavenly Father who loves and supports them unconditionally. This is the Father who knows them inside out and will always be in them and with them. Many little boys do not recognize that the wise, courageous, loving fatherly advice they need, they already have at the core of their being. They don't understand that the Father put it there for them to use when they thought they could not reach him, see him, or be with him. Like a good Father, the heavenly Father has given little boys everything they need to grow into men.

Anger

Feelings of Rejection

If your son has been incarcerated and he has requested that someone come to visit him, and he has had very few visitors, if any, he can be released as an angry young man. Granted, he's put himself in this situation but when he is remorseful for his actions, he is hoping for forgiveness or at least some sort of sympathy. In my case, I attended visitation one time while my son was in juvey. I don't know if the remorse was too great, but I was never allowed to another visitation ever again.

There are no perfect answers and no perfect solutions. All you can do is try. You may have decided to offer tough love instead and leave him to think or maybe you as a mother was there by his side all the way, but the father was absent. Maybe it's just flat out rejection on all levels by the other parent. Feelings of rejection can go much deeper than the surface and this is where counseling can play a pivotal role in addressing issues such as this.

Joblessness

Anytime you have a criminal history and employers can conduct a background check to pull your criminal record, it can be very difficult to find a job. After seeking a job day after day get rejection notices on a continual basis, it can wear anyone down. Unfortunately, this country isn't very forgiving of individuals with a criminal past. There are plenty of other elements that he has to deal with and not having a job is monumental in his eyes because men tend to equate being a man and provider of a family to having a job.

Networking may be helpful in this situation. You would be surprised at how many people you know who may know of another individual with a criminal record and the place they found a job. Many of our peers can guide you to employers who hire ex-offenders. Network with your family and friends to seek direction to employers for your son where they already knows that he is coming with a record. We have to encourage them the best we can because the odds are not stacked in their favor, however, this is where continual prayer comes into play.

This Time It Felt Different

This Time It Felt Different

Chapter 6

This Time It Felt Different

This Time It Felt Different

This Time It Felt Different

As time passed, things improved. I found out that my son had enrolled in our local community college and had begun taking college courses. This did not surprise me. I've always believed all of my children had promise and I instilled the importance of getting a good education at an early age. As a family, we were all working to better ourselves as I too was following suite now working on my Ph.D. and his sister was working on her Pharm.D. studying to be a pharmacist. I was glad to see that he had made the decision to challenge himself mentally by putting himself in a conducive environment that would only benefit him in the long run. I was just praying my way through as a mother and trying to manage my home the best I could. Nonetheless, I still felt like there were matters of the head and matters of the heart. With his head, he was trying by making all the right moves, but I observed his heart was not in the game. It was as if he still had this gray cloud hovering over him that he couldn't shake. He wasn't coming directly home from school, but I was just glad he was coming home. More importantly, I observed that he still was very disconnected. He needed guidance; a guidance that I didn't know how to provide. I never knew what he was thinking, and I wasn't effective in reaching him.

This Time It Felt Different

One evening, it was getting late and I began to call around looking for him. I did not want to think of calling the jail or worse the hospital. As a process of elimination, I ended up calling the county jail. They search their system and I was informed by the authorities that he had been arrested and was in jail awaiting his initial hearing. I was provided with the location, time and date of the hearing. I requested to know why he was arrested. Even after they told me, I didn't know what to think because I didn't know the (level of) seriousness the crime but this time it felt different. I hung up the phone and immediately called a friend who happened to be a judge to inquire what all this meant. He informed me that the penalty was really serious, and he could be sent away for 20 years. I remembered thinking, "Granted, he committed a crime, but it wasn't murder so why was the sentence so steep?" So, right off the bat, I went from looking for my 17-year old son, to finding out he had been arrested, given a hearing date and then being told by someone in the criminal justice profession that the sentence could possibly be 20 years all in a matter of 20 minutes. We had already gone through a lot, but the 20 years component shook me to the core. Before my mind could digest the information and I start freaking out because I felt it coming on quickly, I politely hung up the phone and proceeded to my bedroom, got down on my knees and prayed.

This Time It Felt Different

I was messed up in the head after the news I had just received but this was the first thing I did before making any calls to anyone else. I got on my knees in my bedroom by myself, my mind was racing, and I was scared to death. When I don't have the words to pray, I always pray The Lord's Prayer. I felt that if I'm getting ready to go through a hurricane, as soon as I could, I wanted God in the mix with me. I needed Him and wanted to tell Him first what I had just found out and ask for His help. My mind was in warp speed as I got down on my knees, I was trying to think of all the people who I thought I should call for help. I slowly began to pray... Our Father... which art in Heaven, hallowed be thy name. As I prayed, I was in full focus of every word. I didn't get up right away, I lingered there for a while. I began to notice, the longer I stayed on my knees, my mind slowed down, there was more peace and comfort. I really began to feel a lot better so I stayed on my knees as long as I could. The peace was surprisingly very comfortable and tranquil. It was unlike any peace I had felt before because it was so real. It was like He was carrying me. Nonetheless, I knew I eventually had to get up and make calls. After procrastinating as long as I could, I took the first step to stand and then the next. I observed the minute I got up off my knees, I was back in a very earthly space, all peace was gone, and I was crazy and frantic. I felt the weight of it all over take me as I began to make calls seeking support. The more I heard my own voice explain what was going on with me, the worse I felt. It made everything more real. The pain was unbearable.

"Weeping may endure for a night, but joy comes in the morning."
(Psalms 30:5)

It's Time to Suit Up

If you are going through or have faced a similar situation as mine, its times like this where your faith will be tested the most. It's one thing to go to church every Sunday and worship our God but it's another thing to actually walk the walk. That's when stuff gets real. Even Jesus was not exempt from trials and tribulations so our walk will consist of the same. Get it in your spirit now, you are not alone… you are not alone… you are not alone. Throughout this process, if you feel too overwhelmed or if it gets to be too much, ask Him to relieve some of the pressure. He's already carrying some of the load; believe me, you do not have the full brunt of it. However, if you still find that your load is still too heavy, let him know and he will take on more of it. You will be able to tell the difference but remember, He's walking with you through this.

Guard your heart.

This Time It Felt Different

Let's imagine for a minute on one beautiful day you are out rowing your boat far from the shore and a storm comes unexpectedly. In the middle of all the chaos, water is all around you. It gets splashed in your face sometimes deliberately and sometimes with much force. Nonetheless, no sooner than it hits you, it is wiped away with no meaning. You are still afloat in your storm surrounded by all this water, but you are not sinking because the water is outside of your boat. Your boat only begins to sink when you allow the water to get in the boat.

Even though the chaos is going on all around you, be careful not to let it get in you. You may get hit in the face many times as this is a very hurtful situation. You will find that others who may be close to you may be the ones getting a bucket and throwing water in your boat, however, it's only when you allow the water to stay in your boat that you sink. Let me warn you that you will be surprised by who does the hurting, but it is your job to keep your heart guarded. This means that you may have to leave the room or excuse yourself from conversations. When certain movies come on TV that remind you remotely of your situation and you start to feel bad, excuse yourself. Do what you have to do to protect you and your head space. You have to stay afloat. You do what it takes not to allow your boat to sink. Keep your heart guarded and watch your thoughts. Why?

This Time It Felt Different

When we love someone so very much, and we see them end up in a situation that they've gotten themselves into regardless of whose fault it is, we hurt.

But there is a different kind of hurt when it is your child. This particular pain cuts to the core of your soul. When you make that call to the police department and find out your son has done something to get arrested, stuff gets real. All the questions in your mind start flowing back to back:

- ❖ Why do I have to go through this?
- ❖ What did I do wrong?
- ❖ Did I do anything wrong?
- ❖ What didn't I do?
- ❖ What am I supposed to do?
- ❖ Who do I tell?
- ❖ Can I tell anyone?
- ❖ Lord, where are you??? Again, just stop! It's time to pray.

P – Pray

Take some time, go into that prayer closet or find yourself a space to be alone (or with a loved one if you choose) ... and pray. This is the most important thing you can do because you

This Time It Felt Different

don't know what is to follow and to what extent and depth of the situation or the duration for that matter. Put it all out on the table to Him. You don't know what's going on but God does. He knows where your son is, what he's doing at that moment, if he's scared, safe or confused. The point being, He is with your son. Talk to God and ask Him to take care of your child in your absence. Ask God to look over him and let him learn whatever it may be that He needs him to learn to get him through this situation with the least amount of scars internally and externally.

If you haven't freaked out too much and started making phone calls in a panic, you want to take it to God first.

6 "Do not be anxious about anything but in every situation, by prayer and petition, with thanksgiving, present your requests to God. 7 And the peace of God, which transcends all understanding, will guard your hearts and your minds in Christ Jesus."

Philippians 4:6-7

Take it to God because you are going to need Him to keep you sane and grounded. Ask Him for peace and peace of mind. Whatever is on your heart, talk to Him like you're talking to one of those people that you want to call. If you need to talk to

Him all day long, then you will be having a long conversation that day. The difference will be the peace.

Note: At any time in this process:

- ❖ Pray
- ❖ Listen to what He tells you
- ❖ Do what He tells you to do.
- ❖ Pay attention to what he does; seek His face

Life is about 10% of what happens to you and 90% of how you react. Do try to keep a positive attitude throughout this process despite what is going on around you. Press forward. There is a blessing in this for your son but because you are going through it with him, there is a blessing in this for you too. The bigger the battle, the larger the blessing. Pay attention to what God is doing. You will be able to see Him move if you are paying attention. You are not being punished and he didn't stop loving you or your son nowhere in this process; He's doing what a loving father would do by taking control of the situation. Typically, God would make a way financially to get bills paid or come up with money to take care of certain situations. I was paying attention and God made it so obviously clear that this particular time when my son was arrested, God set it up where all of my finances were strapped. There were no

This Time It Felt Different

resources available on any level. He showed me that it was very deliberate and that it was all His doing. He was clear. He was God and He needed me to step back and not take care of this. He showed me that He knew if I had the means, I would pay whatever the cost to correct the situation. He showed me His face. If this is happening to you, it's no coincidence. Let go and let God.

R – Do Your Own Research

I remember calling the authorities and they were utilizing terms that I did not understand such as misdemeanor and felony. I instantly knew that this information was critical, and I would need help. I took a pen and paper and wrote down all the information I could get. I utilized this information and began keeping a log. It was this information that I later could provide to my attorney who could cross reference if needed to confirm if the information was accurate or explain to me in layman's terms the meaning.

An arrest means that one has been taken into custody and they no longer have the freedom to leave on their own accord. Prior to speaking with the authorities, be prepared to write down everything that they tell you and get names of the individuals that you spoke with so that you can later reference them if the need arises. Find out exactly what happened at the scene as it relates to your son or how do you go about obtaining a police report.

In my case, I was eventually shown the police report from the public defender who was assigned to represent us. There are still other questions you can ask the authorities while you have them on the phone such as:

- ❖ What is his current location? – Where is he currently being held and how long will he be there?
- ❖ Has he been booked or processed? – This is the process of providing authorities with his personal information to include being finger printed and photographed.
- ❖ When is his court hearing? – There will be an initial court hearing/arraignment soon after the arrest. Find out if the initial hearing has been set? If so, find out the time and place of the hearing. In court they will refer to your son as the Defendant. This is where the Judge will ask if the defendant would like a Public Defender or if he would like to hire a private attorney? It is during the hearing that the Judge will read the charges and ask, "How do you plead, guilty or not guilty?" If your son has already had his initial hearing, find out when the next hearing will be scheduled.

This Time It Felt Different

- Was there a bail set? Bail is an amount of money that can be paid for your son to be released that is set by the judge, however, it is mandatory that he returns for the next appointed court hearing. If you choose to pay the established bail amount set, your son will be released temporarily. If you choose not to pay the bail, he will wait in jail until the court hearing.
- When did the arrest take place? – What is the time frame? This lets you know how much time has passed since he has been incarcerated.
- What is the place of the incident? – Was it in a store? A house? A car? Just so that you will know the location.
- How many other people were involved or was it a solo act? This may work in your son's favor or not at all.
- How many charges are there and what are they? This information is imperative. There is a difference between 2 charges and 7 charges.
- Was it a misdemeanor or felony? – A felony is more serious than a misdemeanor so find out the level in the classification of the charges. (We will discuss in detail later).
- Did he confess to anything? – Did he admit to the charges? This is critical information to the case as it will

determine if your son will be "innocent until proven guilty" in your favor.

❖ Were there any witnesses? – Is there anyone who will testify as a witness to the crime? This can either hurt or help your son's case.

A - Assess Confidants To Identify Your Support System

After you finish praying, conducting your research and collecting information from your own internal investigation, this is the time to make the phone calls but not just calls to anyone. Use discernment about who you call to confide in because you will need the support later. People who you thought were your "friends" may be the ones talking about you later in a derogatory way. This is not the time when you are being hit with something so hurtful and sensitive of this magnitude that you need to give fuel to your haters. Once you've confided in your friends, you cannot take the information back; it's out there. More importantly, you don't know how long this process will take, so be selective. You will need a support system which will be a very small group of people. If by chance you happen to be connected with someone who works in the system, and you think you can confide in them and they can provide you with accurate information, I would put them on the list of people to call.

Call your closest family member or friend that:

- ❖ You can trust
- ❖ Confide in
- ❖ Who will give you the support that you need
- ❖ Who will listen
- ❖ Who won't judge you
- ❖ Who will pray with and/or for you

Take a minute to think this through. This person should be able to calm you and help you to sort out all the information you have thus far. This person should be someone who is sensitive because emotions will be running high. I don't recommend calling a group of people in one sitting because the more people involved, the potential for you to go crazy with all the questions increases and you don't need the pressure. When you have concrete information and you've strengthened yourself through prayer, you are more equipped to deal with other people inquiring into your business. Remember, you are in control of who knows what's going on with you in your house. People don't generally know your business unless you tell them so again, be selective. This isn't one of those times to

This Time It Felt Different

call everybody frantically because many people gossip, and you don't need this when you're hurting.

As time passes, you will find out who's in your corner and who is not. Learn early who you need to keep close and who you need to keep a limit on the conversations. Keep only the information which will be useful, helpful and what you need. This information will come from spirit-filled people in the form of something biblically-based. You will find yourself thinking about this message long after the conversation with this friend is over. You will find that they strengthen you. You have calmness when speaking to this messenger and you will want to speak to them again for that reassurance. They leave you with a sense of peace. You know in your heart God is using them to get a word to you. This is the person you need to surround yourself with the most. You are so much stronger than you think. You can handle it because He's already given you everything you need to weather through this storm.

I can do all things through [a] Christ who strengthens me.
Philippians 4:13

This Time It Felt Different

For me, I considered myself very selective in who I confided in to the point that most of my core family did not find out until months later what I was dealing with. Most people have one individual that they can confide in about anything. This is where I messed up and brought more harm on myself. The one person that I thought was in my corner turned out to be the very person who later used my situation to hurt me. When the opportunity presented itself, they used this circumstance while the wound was very open to pour in the salt. You don't know how long this storm will last and it is support that you need the most. A word from the wise, if they have not supported you in the past, then they will not be a good candidate to support you now.

Yield - Contact Your Attorney

Seek advice from any attorneys that you may know or who are highly recommended. Many attorneys will offer free consultation services in effort to service you as a client. If you have the financial means to hire a private attorney, go for it! This may ultimately end up costing several thousands of dollars in the end depending on the severity of the case which equates to how long the case will last. However, if you don't have access to money immediately to obtain counsel, at least speak with a professional in the field, who can answer all of your questions and provide you with some insight.

Remember, I sought out a friend who was a judge that worked the bench. Surely a judge was knowledgeable. After explaining everything I had been told from the authorities, he informed me that my son may get 20 years. There was no life lost or anything remotely close, but I hung up the phone confused and devastated. I cried myself to sleep that night with this on my heart. Can you imagine??? He was wrong. So I reiterate, be careful that you get counsel from a reputable and knowledgeable source that will provide you with accurate information.

Depending on the case, after the initial hearing, your attorney will at some point meet with the prosecuting attorney in effort to come up with a plea bargain. This is a more lenient sentence that is agreed upon between the two for the alleged charges. If an agreement cannot be made, in some cases, the decision can be made by the judge or the case can go to trial that will involve a jury. If the jury finds your son not guilty, he can go home. However, if the jury comes up with a guilty verdict, they are then sentenced at the jury or judge's discretion. In my situation, I'm sure our public defender spoke with the prosecuting attorney and the judge made the ultimate decision regarding my son's case.

There is also the option that the offence can potentially come with the minimum of an additional monetary fine, community service and/or probation and if a probation violation occurs, a suspended sentence can be reinstated whereby returning to jail is possible. Probation guidelines are adhered to very strictly by courts. If your son feels that he has not received fair justice, your attorney can submit an appeal but be prepared for a long and lengthy fight within the judicial system. Seek legal counsel for additional information and clarification.

Questions For The Public Defender

Chapter 7

Questions For The Public Defender

Questions For The Public Defender

Questions For The Public Defender

Unfortunately, unless you have a private attorney which can be quite costly, maneuvering through the judicial system is a very helpless state of existence in the sense that very little is in your control. Throughout this process, I had one private attorney but primarily, a series of public defenders were assigned to my case randomly with multiple styles of practicing law. I never knew when they would change or the reason. I just had to jump in and bring them up to speed on the history of my sons case and pray for the best at each hearing. I had to come to grips with the fact that my son was now in this judicial system. My responsibilities in life did not stop as I was trying to still deal with this situation the best way I could. I decided to fight and take the responsibility on the outside to do what was necessary in effort to help my son on the inside. My goal was to prohibit the system from keeping my son for an extensively long time past what was required of him. I felt like I was fighting the devil and I treated it as such.

I was told that he was a ward of the state; his fate is in a judge's hands and we were given a court representative, a Public Defender speaking on my son's behalf. The concern is that most Public Defenders have an average of more than 100 cases at any given time, so they are clearly overworked and many working on a teacher's salary. This means you are

Questions For The Public Defender

navigating through the system with an overworked attorney and a good probability that the judge has gotten immune to his/her cases as well. To merely say that you are placed in a very vulnerable position is an understatement.

As your son's case gets extended over time for various reasons, with each new Public Defender, I had a new set of questions. This case was never far from my mind. Throughout the day, as questions came to mind, I kept a little notebook on me to log my questions so that I would not forget them when I spoke with council. I encourage you to ask as many questions that come to your mind. Some of mine were as follows:

How will I know if there has been a continuance (a postponed hearing)?

If there is a continuance and it occurs prior a scheduled hearing, request in advance from your public defender that you be notified. Maybe they'll notify you, maybe they won't but at least you can ask. If there is any planning or traveling involved, this information can be helpful and save on cost even if you have to travel downtown to the courthouse. Nonetheless, if the hearing has been continued or any other additional changes to the case, you want to be updated so make that clear upfront.

Have you spoken to my son yet?

Questions For The Public Defender

You want your public defender/attorney to speak with your son as soon as possible to find out the details. Once I found out who was assigned to my sons' case, I called, left messages and borderline harassed until I received a response. I made it clear that this case had to be taken seriously. I wanted someone to go and see my son as soon as possible. I could get my questions answered but I didn't want him having questions and no one to answer them.

Your son will also have the option to complete a Verbal Authorization Form which means that your son gives his authorization for release of information of discussions he had with his attorney to you. This will waive Attorney/Client privilege. You want as much information as possible so that you can plan what to do next or educate yourself on next steps. More than likely, you can expect to hear from your son but understand, ALL CALLS ARE BEING RECORDED. It may take several days after the arrest occurred but hopefully, you will get a call from your son soon after the arrest. Best case scenario would be if he allows, you can visit him.

What do you foresee happening?

There are no guarantees but since your attorney will have more experience with the system than you, it will not hurt to get their point of view based on their past experiences with cases like this or judges they've encountered. You just are asking to get a feel for what potentially may happen in the future based on what they've seen. This opinion is just an educated guess not fact, but it can help provide guidance in terms of a glimpse of what may happen in the future.

In addition, your attorney may have insight as it relates to the judges. Because they work in this field, many of the attorneys already know the temperament of the judge if they find out prior to the hearing who will be working the bench. Every bit of knowledge helps.

What (if anything) do you know that I don't know because I don't like surprises?

This question was critical for me. With each Public Defender, my responses varied. By asking this question, you are giving your attorney an opportunity to provide you with additional information that you may not be aware of at that time. At the same time, you are letting him know that you would rather know upfront any potential derogatory information that can be harmful. You would rather be informed in advance than get in court and watch the bottom fall out unexpectedly. You are making it clear that you would

Questions For The Public Defender

much rather be very knowledgeable and informed rather than only have surface information.

What do you have in mind for this case? What deal are you trying to make (if any)?

More often than not, the prosecutors and the attorneys know each other. The best way to look at this relationship would be how you view your co-workers at your job. Having said that, conversations are prone to occur, and deals are possibly made prior to your son even walking into the courtroom. Although they may (not) be close buddies, they have more likely than not, come across each other in the court room or in passing and are very familiar with each other's work. You can discuss with your son's attorney in advance the possibilities of deal options so that he will know in advance what you are willing to accept and what will be deal breakers. He will ultimately make the deal, but the bottom line is that you want your voice to be heard and you want to be a part of the negotiating process.

If the attorneys are going to have discussion regarding you son's case and are in negotiating process, prior to going to court, you can ask questions to the Public Defender such as:

Questions For The Public Defender

- ❖ What were his/her thoughts about what can take place.
- ❖ What options were they planning to propose to the prosecuting attorney that may be acceptable in the court?
- ❖ What conclusion were they seeking?

The goal of the conversation is to participate in the decision-making process to come up with an acceptable solution on behalf of your son. Nonetheless, keep in mind, the judge makes the decision based on what is heard. Your purpose for asking all the questions is where you won't be blind-sided and that you are knowledgeable of all options on the table.

How do you see this case going?

Sometimes attorneys have seen similar cases and know the judge or know the "Sentencing Chart" that will be utilized in court. Each state has a Sentencing Chart that outlines for you not only if time served is mandatory, but how much is required. Finding out from them in advance an accurate account of time to be served can potentially soften the blow in a sentencing. They are educating you on how your case would typically play out in the courtroom. This will allow you to mentally prepare for what is to come.

Questions For The Public Defender

Mental preparation will always be helpful. Try to be proactive and get information as it relates to the Sentencing Chart prior to the hearing so that you will know what you're up against.

Follow the Holy Spirits lead.

Allow the Holy Spirit to guide you. When you hear that little voice like a whisper tell you that something isn't right, please listen. If you feel that you are not in tuned with the Holy Spirit, God gave you instinct. Use your gut. For instance, if your instincts are telling you that your public defender/lawyer is not looking out for your best interest or he's just going through the motions, very inattentive and very uninvolved, seek new representation. I cannot stress how important of a role this will play in the outcome. Do not disregard the Holy Spirit when He is clearly speaking to you at any time during this process. When you feel in your spirit something isn't right, that's a big indicator that something is not right.

How long do you think this process will be?

You can ask this question and your Sentencing Chart will give you some kind of indication of how long your son may be incarcerated based on the level of the offense. Initially, I went numb and that was all I thought about was the date of release. I thought the situation would be over on that date, but I was wrong. More often than not, after the sentence, the judge may assign a probationary time period with additional guidelines. This is equivalent to an extended sentence. The same clock is still ticking because it still is not over.

All you know is that it feels like this process will never be over. I encourage you. This too shall pass. Surprisingly for me, asking the attorneys all the questions I felt that I needed to in order to make me feel better helped me tremendously. I was thankful that they were understanding and patient with me once I developed a relationship. You do need some peace of mind in this process. In other words, it's comforting to have a date that you can look forward to for closure. This date turns into GOLD. Compare for yourself this date with the sentencing chart to ensure that they line up.

I EMPHASIZE THAT YOU ASK YOUR ATTORNEY:

- EVERYTHING YOU NEED TO KNOW,
- AS MANY QUESTIONS AS YOU FEEL YOU NEED TO ASK,

Questions For The Public Defender

- AND AS OFTEN AS YOU NEED IN ORDER TO MAKE YOU FEEL BETTER AND GIVE YOU PEACE OF MIND.

Is he eligible to qualify to be released where he can come home with the ankle monitor? If so, what programs do they have and what is the cost per month?

You want your son home as soon as possible; this is the goal. Depending on the seriousness of the case, an ankle monitor, or bracelet may (not) be an option but it will not hurt to ask. If he is eligible, again, there will be a cost associated with utilizing this system and it could be expensive. Know that it varies per state depending on which company is contracted with the state for their services.

Questions For The Public Defender

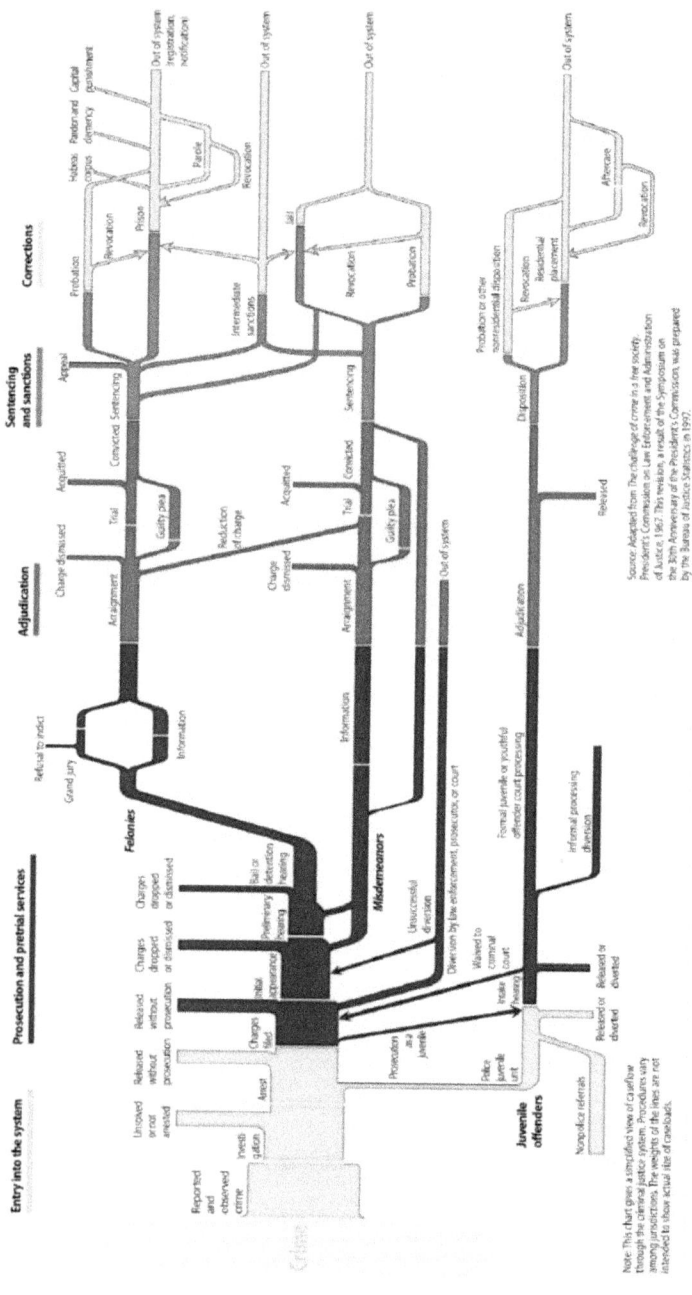

~ 108 ~

Questions For The Public Defender

What is the role of the Prosecutor's Office?

The use of knowledge is power. If your son already has a record on file, expect that the Prosecuting Attorney will use this information against your son to state his/her case. You want to know what your opponent knows so that you won't get into court and get blind-sided. The sole purpose of the Prosecutor's Office presence in the courtroom will be to prosecute your son. Period. More than likely, there is a probability that you will grow not to like them, however, they are doing a job.

I can recall sitting directly behind the team of Prosecutor's as they were totally oblivious that they were discussing how to maneuver to get this young man off to jail right in front of his mother. It was like watching a bad scene in a movie whereby the good guys were fighting to keep my son safe against the bad guys who wanted to send him away for their gain and profit. When the arguing ended, the judge spoke and I heard the prosecuting team say to each other, "YES!!! GOT him!"

Sentencing

As I watched them celebrate amongst themselves, I sat devastated and helpless. My son would not be coming home with me. The mood in the courtroom had definitely changed. I didn't want to cry because I didn't want to embarrass my son by making a scene. I had prepared a written letter for the Judge so that she would take into account that he was a young man who had people who loved him.

Penalties: Felony vs. Misdemeanor

Penalties: Felony vs. Misdemeanor

Chapter 8

Penalties: Felony vs. Misdemeanor

Penalties: Felony vs. Misdemeanor

Penalties: Felony vs. Misdemeanor

There are multiple levels of misdemeanors and felonies that determine the sentencing time to be served.

Regardless if it is a misdemeanor or a felony, a paper trail is being developed in the criminal justice system that will be permanent. This criminal record can be utilized against your son by the prosecutor's office 10, 20 or 30 years from now if the record is never expunged.

Pay special attention to if the offense is a violation of state law vs. federal law. Time issued under state law is different from time issued under federal law. The penalties for state laws vary from state to state. When you find out if the penalty will be classified as a misdemeanor or a felony, it will be to your advantage to go online to research the applicable penalties for your state. You will also need the category of the offence of the misdemeanor or felony. By state, you are seeking to find the maximum time to be served and the maximum amount of the penalty. For instance, in the State of Indiana, the prosecutors who represent the state utilize a sentencing chart in court that outlines what the category is for each offense. It defined the minimum and maximum length of time allowed for each category of criminal offense. This chart provides the mandatory sentencing requirements per offense. Each state may vary. In the state of Indiana requirements are as follows.

Penalties: Felony vs. Misdemeanor

Misdemeanors

Misdemeanor offenses have a maximum penalty of up to 1 year in jail.

Class A Misdemeanors

A class A misdemeanor is the most serious type of misdemeanor, punishable by up to one year in jail and a fine of up to $5,000. (Ind. Code Ann. § 35-50-3-2.) Possession of up to 30 grams of marijuana is an example of a class A misdemeanor.

Class B Misdemeanors

Class B misdemeanors are punishable by up to 180 days in jail and a fine of up to $1,000.

(Ind. Code Ann. § 35-50-3-3.) For example, public intoxication is a class B misdemeanor.

Class C Misdemeanors

A class C misdemeanor is punishable by up to 60 days in jail and a fine of up to $500. (Ind. Code Ann. § 35-50-3-4.) Driving under the influence (DUI) is a class C misdemeanor if

Penalties: Felony vs. Misdemeanor

it is the person's first DUI offense and the person's blood alcohol content (BAC) is over .08 but less than .15.

Class A Misdemeanors	Up to 1 year in jail	Fines reaching $5,000
Class B Misdemeanors	Up to 180 days in jail	Fines reaching $1,000
Class C Misdemeanors	Up to 60 days in jail	Fines reaching $500

Statutes of Limitations

Misdemeanors have fairly short statutes of limitations (time limits) during which the prosecutor must file criminal charges. Once the crime is committed, the statute of limitations begins to "run." When the statute of limitations has run out, the crime can no longer be prosecuted. Ref: IC 35-50-3-1

Felonies

Penalties: Felony vs. Misdemeanor

Far more serious than misdemeanors, felonies are punishable by terms in the state prison system and can result in significant prison time as well as hefty fines. Judges also have more leeway in sentencing for felonies. Felonies are split into 5 classes (Class A, B, C, or D with murder getting its own classification. In Indiana, a felony is any crime that carries a penalty of more than one year in prison.

Class A Felonies

A class A felony in Indiana is punishable by 20 to 50 years' imprisonment and a fine of up to $10,000. (Ind. Code Ann. § 35-50-2-4.) For example, aggravated rape (rape by deadly force or with the use of a weapon) is a class A felony.

Class B Felonies

As the states vary, in Indiana, class B felonies are punishable by six to 20 years in prison and a fine of up to $10,000. (Ind. Code Ann. § 35-50-2-5.) Aggravated battery (causing serious injury to another) is a class B felony.

Class C Felonies

A conviction for a class C felony can result in two to eight years' imprisonment and a fine of up to

Penalties: Felony vs. Misdemeanor

$10,000. (Ind. Code Ann. § 35-50-2-6.) Vehicle theft is an example of a class C felony.

Class D Felonies

Class D felonies are "wobblers," crimes that can be either a felony or a misdemeanor, depending on how the crime is charged and, sometimes, how the judge decides to treat a conviction. Class D felonies are punishable by at least six months in jail (a misdemeanor sentence) or as much as three years in prison (a felony sentence), as well as a fine of up to $10,000. (Ind. Code Ann. § 35-50-2-7.) For example, battery that causes injury to a child under the age of 14 is a class D felony.

Class D Felony	6 months- 3 years in prison
Class C Felony	2-8 years in prison
Class B Felony	6-20 years in prison
Class A Felony	20-50 years in prison

Penalties: Felony vs. Misdemeanor

Murder	45 years in prison- life, or death penalty

You may also be sentenced to fines reaching $10,000 if convicted of any felony charge. Ref: Indiana IC 35-50-2

A Long-Term Consequence of Drug Related Arrest

Out of all the charges, drug charges are one of the most serious. Black (2015) states, "America has the longest first-time drug offense sentences of developed nations." Dimon states (2014), "If convicted, a first-time drug offense carries a sentence of 5-10 years. In other developed countries, that sentence would be six months of jail time, if any at all."

One of the consequences directly related to the criminal justice system is obtaining financial aid for college tuition. Please be aware that if in the long run, your son pulls it together and decides he wants to go to college, in order to receive student loans or financial aid, he will need to submit a FASFA (Financial Aid Student Financial Aid). There is one question on the FASFA application that inquiries about getting arrested and they want to know specifically if the arrest was drug related.

Penalties: Felony vs. Misdemeanor

Being arrested for any drug related offense is one of the stipulations that may prohibit him from receiving financial aid for college unless you are paying cash. In other words, if he was arrested at 18 years old, serves his time and at the age of 20, he decides he wants to go off to college. You proceed and complete the FASFA for him to receive student loans. If his arrest is not drug related, he can more than likely proceed and go off to college and live in a dorm. For drug-related offenses, there is a possibility that you may be denied for financial aid.

The worst-case scenario for any parent is if the courts decides that your child will not be allowed to come home and sentences him to do time. The judge may (not) order that your son is moved to another facility if it is for an extended stay other than being sent to jail. If the law that was broken is a state law, they will move him to either a state prison or if a federal law was broken, he will be sent to federal prison.

You can be present in the courtroom to see exactly what is happening or find out where your son is being sent and the reason(s). If you are not able to be present when this occurs, you can request that your public defender contact you and inform you of exactly what has happened in the courtroom, what it all means, where they are sending him and what your next steps can be However, if you are present, you may (not)

Penalties: Felony vs. Misdemeanor

be allowed to speak before the judge on your child's behalf. The purpose of your presentation will be to insert a human element into the courtroom so that the judge will understand that there are people who love your son in effort to sway the judge. However, keep in mind that they have a predetermined sentencing chart that accounts for time to be served based on the various offenses. Again, educate yourself on what this chart entails for your state but be prepared to speak on your son's behalf regardless.

Your son may (not) have to serve all the time listed. There are several factors that can play a key role (i.e. First-time offenders, prison overcrowding, the severity of the crime committed). For state prisons, time served is 50% of the sentence given in court. Each state varies. It will be very difficult to hear confirmation that your son will not be returning home anytime soon. For the strongest of us, this is hard and very painful.

The judge may (not) allow you to speak. Afterwards, the judge will deliberate on all the findings and issue a sentence. This very well may be one of the harder days throughout this process because you will now have a timeframe where the clock starts ticking. I cried and I prayed, and I prayed, and I cried.

Penalties: Felony vs. Misdemeanor

This is one time in your life where your faith in God will be tested. Try to again surround yourself with people you know who will be supportive of you and just be a listening ear and when needed, a shoulder to cry on. This may be when you feel the most helpless. After going to court and possibly paying for attorneys, you just want this to be over. You are not alone. Find people or be open to people that God sends your way who may have a similar story or have gone through a similar experience. This can be the greatest comfort is having someone who knows your pain first hand that you can confide in. They may end up being your biggest support system.

Don't go to your brother's house in the day of your disaster: better is a neighbor who is than a distant brother.

Proverbs 27: 10

In the Meantime

In the meantime, it feels like time can't go any slower. A day can feel like a week. While your son is away paying his debt to society, it is very important that you keep busy. Keep your mind occupied. This is where you stand strong in your faith knowing that God is still in control and He knows what He is doing. Do not allow your mind to play tricks on you; this is just the devil playing with your head. God is there with your son and sees all. Just continue to lift your son up in prayer and ask for His protection and God to provide your son with wisdom. I didn't have any male mentors for my son, but God worked it out where he was surrounded by a group of older men who could stand in that void for him and provide him with the guidance that he needed. I could tell a difference in him through his letters and when I spoke to him. I was grateful for what God was doing with my son's spirit regardless of his environment. I'm not saying that he was away on vacation, don't get me wrong, I'm sure he saw a lot of awful things, but I do believe that all men locked up are not bad people. I would ask God to lead angels to your son even while he's incarcerated. Believe me, God can use anybody. While in the meantime – Trust

Trust Changes Your Perspective

Excerpt on Trust in Until Today

by Iyanla Vanzant

Why don't you just admit that you have absolutely no idea what's going on? The only thing required for your enlightment for your blessings to flow, is for you to figure out that you don't have to know what is going on. All you have to do is trust. Everything else is something that you make up in your own mind just to give yourself something to do or not do.

Penalties: Felony vs. Misdemeanor

If you really want to give your mind something to do, think about the beauty that surrounds you. Think about the trees, flowers and all of the little animals that may not have dreams, visions and schedules, but seem to make it through each day just fine. Think about how much you have grown in your life. Think about how much you have learned in your life. Think about how far you have come, even when you weren't quite sure of where you were headed or what you were going to do when you got to where you are. Think about all the near misses you have had. Then think about all the connections you have made. Think about all the second chances you have had. Then think about all the chances you did not take. If you just have to have something to think about, think about the glorious wonder that lie is, has been and continues to be. Then ask yourself why you think that you should know, could know, are supposed to know what's going on? Think about all the good stuff that has happened to you that you didn't know was going to happen. Then ask yourself why you are so fixed on knowing when trusting seems to have paid off so well, so far?

5 Trust in the Lord with all your heart and lean not on your own understanding;

6 in all your ways submit to him,

and he will make your paths straight

Proverbs 3:5-6

The Cost Of Prison

Chapter 9

The Cost Of Prison

The Cost Of Prison

The Cost Of Prison

While you are in the meantime, add your son to the budget because it is going to cost you. The criminal justice system is an 80 BILLION-dollar industry. Worth Rises, a non-for-profit company out of New York, NY released a comprehensive report in April 2019 called The Prison Industrial Complex: Mapping Private Sector Players. It discusses how government agencies collaborate with for-profit businesses who make their money off of those with the least. The 2.2 million people incarcerated in the U.S. and their support networks are both vulnerable to corporate abuse. Over half of the 80 billion is spent by government agencies who are paying thousands of dollars for vendors who provide services for the criminal judicial services. Among many others, they are healthcare providers, food suppliers, and commissary retailers.

This report also exposes roughly 4000 corporations that profited from mass incarceration of our nation's most vulnerable communities. This figure has increased by 800 additional companies just since last year. The Executive Director, Bianca Tylek explained: "Before this report, many of the companies involved in the prison industrial complex flew below the radar, often intentionally to avoid the headline risk that comes with profiting off mass incarceration today."

The Cost Of Prison

A few of the companies who are benefiting now or have previously benefited in the past directly or indirectly are: Attenti, GEO Group, CoreCivic/Avalon, Turner Construction and Equivant. If you don't recognize those, maybe you will recognize these: Target (has utilized suppliers that rely on prison labor) Amazon, Victoria Secret (in the 1990's, they used prison labor to sew clothes making 45 cents an hour), Whole Foods Market, Walmart (says they won't sell products made with prison labor but contracts with companies who do), Microsoft, Starbucks (has used prison labor to package coffee sold in its stores paying 23 cents an hour) Nintendo, AT&T (inmates used to man its call centers; paid $2 a day), BP (hired Louisiana prison inmates to clean up the oil spill; the workers were not paid at all), Unicor, Dell, Eddie Bauer, Kmart (jeans manufactured by prisoners), Boeing, Macy's, Wendy's (hired inmates to process beef), Verizon (uses inmates in call centers), McDonald's (uniforms manufactured by prisoners), Revlon Group, JCPenney, Sprint Corporation (uses inmates in call centers), Honda Motor Company (has paid inmates 25-40 cents an hour), Fruit of the Loom, Intel, Nordstrom, Motorola, Koch Industries, American Airlines, and the list goes on.

I was stunned to find out how much I would be charged just to hear my son's voice. Companies like Securus and Keefe

The Cost Of Prison

are charging as much as $25 for every 15-minute phone call and $6 for a $20 deposit."

Let's start with the salary while behind bars. Inmates earn as little as 9-12 cents per hour, so they are not able to provide for themselves. This salary has not been increased in decades although the items to be purchased have been increased significantly. So, when they ask for money, they do need it. There are a few things you can do to provide assistance to make life a little easier despite the circumstances:

Put Money on the Books

When your son is relocated to a new place, there are a few necessities that he will need. He may identify what that is to you. These essentials cost money so when he first arrives and is getting situated, he will need the toothpaste, toothbrush, etc. The cost for these necessities will not be the prices we pay at our local Walmart. The prices he will pay will be inflated significantly. If he doesn't have what he needs, there may be an option for him to rent them for a daily rental fee. But now, he will be in the negative so when you do send money, that fee will have to be paid. It would be helpful for you to place "money on the books" for him to decide how the money should be allocated. Your son will more than likely provide you with a number to a company that will provide a service to

The Cost Of Prison

allow you to make deposits. He will let you know what he needs and the service for you to sign up with to pay the money so that it can be transferred to him. Depending on the state, most states utilize a company called JPay. The fees can be as high as 35-45%. I can recall each time I needed to send him $30 but having to pay $50 instead. What happened to the other $20?

Wagner states (2014), JPay and other prison bankers collect tens of millions of dollars every year from inmates' families in fees for basic financial services. JPay handled nearly 7 million transactions in 2013, generating well over $50 million in revenue. It was expected to transfer more than $1 billion in 2014. JPay says it has grown to provide money transfers to more than 1.5million offenders in 35 states, or nearly 70 percent of the inmates in U.S. prisons. The parent company of JPay is Securus Technologies, a national prison telecommunications corporation and Securus has a 30-year contract with non-other than Bank of America.

Put Money on the Phone

Very similar to putting money on the books; there is another service for the phone. More than likely, the service provider will be… you guess it – Jpay. They have pay phones that will be made available, however, they cost money. When you put money on the phone, there is an initial fee taken out

The Cost Of Prison

just for sending the money and the remainder is what he has to work with. Typically, that charge is $6.95 per call and an additional charge per minute. If the call is disconnected for some unknown reason and you call back, it will be another $6.95 fee to make the call again. I was often left asking what happened to my $14? Just like putting money on the books, you are also allowed to place prepaid funds in advance that are debited to his account to utilize the phone in the future.

"When inmates can't afford to maintain contact with the outside world, they are less equipped to transition smoothly to civilian life" says Wagner (2014). It is my hope that changes are made on the national level soon. Cohen states (2019), "Connecticut may soon be the first state in the nation to make calls from prison free for incarcerated people and their families, following on the heels of New York City, which became the first city to do so last year. In April 2019, Connecticut moved forward with H.B. No. 6714. My prayer is that other states begin to follow suite.

Send Letters

Writing in a journal or writing letters to your son can be very therapeutic. I chose to write to my son for several reasons.

(1) Love

The Cost Of Prison

I needed him to know that I still loved him as his mother. This was a low point in his life, and he needed someone who loved him unconditionally to stand with him. He needed to know that I still cared about him and his well- being. There is no way for me to know or imagine what it is like being housed where he was living so I wanted to do what I could to show him that I support him.

(2) Inclusion

I wanted him to still be as knowledgeable as to what went on in our home as if he was still living there. Every activity, trip, conference, event that our family experienced, I informed him of what was currently happening and all that was upcoming to keep him in the loop. I asked for his input many times because I wanted him to know his opinion mattered because he was still a part of our family.

(3) Therapy

I found in writing my letters to my son, it was helpful to me as a release. I had so much pinned up animosity in me because it is a LOT to digest when your son has to live some place he does not want to be. We were able to communicate and say things that we probably would not have said in person. We had discussions about his father and what happened in my marriage that he had always been curious about, but it had gone unsaid. Our relationship improved immensely to where we actually became good friends.

I tried to make sure that he was getting a letter the majority of the time he was there. I wanted to keep them coming at least every other day. There were times he would get 2 letters in one day due to backlog or he would get a letter and had not completed the letter he had opened. I was long winded in my writing. I wanted to document our life to him. He was very into sports, so I sent sports news. I wanted him to have something, a distraction to take him out of his environment and into our world if only for a minute, mission accomplished.

Visitation Possibilities

You will have the opportunity to visit your son. If he will allow you to come and see him, go and visit him if you can. I'm sure it would me a lot to him. There are multiple categories of visitation so I would research to find what is available at his facility and see what suits your family circumstances best.

(4) To Shift the Focus

The battle is in the mind. Troubles don't last always. This is just one chapter in your life and it is temporary. Just knowing that he will be coming home one day brings comfort. Keep

The Cost Of Prison

your focus on the goal whatever your goal may be. If you don't have a goal, come up with one. My goal was to help my son to get past all of this, living a productive life with goals of his own. I also asked God to make Satan pay. I wanted Satan to pay BAD for messing with my son and our family so keep focus on the outcome that you want to see. Talk to God about it, let Him know your heart and watch what He does. This too shall pass.

I also wanted to shift the focus off of my son's circumstances to life on the outside. When he's reading, his mind is on the content of the material he's reading. If I can remove him from his circumstances if only for one minute, then that's one less minute of hell that he has to endure. This is why I provided as many details of my life as possible. The point was that when he came home, I didn't want him to miss a beat. I didn't want him to be in the dark about what we did and places we had visited in his absence. I wanted him to travel with us if but only in his mind. Providing him with an escape, this small escape I believe will help him with his day because he now has something else to think about other than what he sees.

Release

Release

Chapter 10

Release

Release

Release

As time passes, you learn to smile again and eventually you learn to laugh. As with anything, time helps with the adjustment process. There is no doubt that you are much stronger now in your spiritual walk than you were when this journey first began. God has been working with you and taught you a lot about your strength, power, patience and love. You know that you are strong without a doubt.

In some states, there are programs that were established to prepare inmates for release. Some of the programs prepare inmates for life on the outside with at least one year to the release date. We know what the programs are supposed to do like prepare you for job readiness and provide the soft skills necessary to get and keep the job. However, the problem is that because there is little accountability, this program becomes just another job for many who work in the system. You will be allowed to go out during the day to find employment, but you have to return to sleep at the facility in the evening. Like many programs offered in the system, they are not closely monitored, there are no assessments to provide the public with success records and there is no real data on effective rehabilitation long term. The criminal justice system has just become a place to house individuals for a certain length of time until it is time for their release. There is a lack of research to determine the efficacy of the many programs offered while inmates are incarcerated. However, the rehabilitation to inmates are minimal and we have this data based on the recidivism rate across this country that remains consistently high and I do not believe this is a coincidence.

After they are allowed to seek employment and work on jobs for a year, still returning to the facility in evening, you are allowed to see your son during this time frame because they are also given passes. This was a blessing for (3) main reasons for us: (1) this allowed us to be together as a family again (2) my son could have my cooking again (3) my son could take baths. Granted, he had a curfew, but these were just things that were priceless that we took for granted.

After the year is up and the release date comes, he still may not be allowed to come straight home contingent on what was determined in his sentencing. He may be on probation and be sent to a group home for a period of time. The program for him to find employment is also to transition him into the group home. What they don't tell you is that there are multiple layers in this release process.

In this group home, he will be required to get a job within a set timeframe (if he still does not have one yet) because he will have to pay rent to be in this group home. There will be someone that he has to report to in the group home and he will continue to have a curfew. The layers will include a psychological adjustment for the family and for him.

He also may be dealing with his own personal issues because for him, these layers can be a residue of emotions and beliefs of his struggle. This struggle can include feelings of resentment and in some cases rejection while he has been away, joblessness, awkwardness in reconnecting to people who are typically close and readjusting to life on the outside. I want to give you a heads up on a few things that you may encounter as this chapter of your life comes to a close.

Prepare the family and the house

It would be beneficial to speak with the family in advance to discuss how things may change. Mentally prepare the family for all the dynamics of the house to change because your son will be moving back home. More than likely, your son will need his own space just like everyone else so be prepared. There is a mental adjustment that needs to take place with all family members so the earlier this process can begin, the better for the transition. Things changed when he left and everyone had to adjust, so now, this will be the readjustment process for getting use to him being home. Keep in mind, everyone has grown but in different ways.

He won't be the same; give him time to readjust

No one may feel the brunt of weirdness more than your son. It's no different than if you moved out of your home for an extended length of time and you move back to your family. It takes time to get readjusted so allow him time to do that. He will come to realize that since he's been gone, life continued on. It's kind of hard to see that everyone went on with their lives because they had to and also because that was the thing to do. It will take time for him to figure out where he fits in this equation.

Additionally, you may observe that he stopped maturing and growing. He may still be in that same head space (mentally) when he left. You may observe that for him, time stopped to a certain degree. Understand that life didn't stop for you, but it really did for him and he can't get that time back so be compassionate as far as this is concerned. Just allow him to get readjusted now. That will be enough. There are a lot of things on his mind now like where and how will he get a job. Most men are natural providers by nature. It means everything for them to be the caretaker in their household. For some, that's

Release

what defines them as a man. It would be helpful to network prior to him coming home to see if you can help find a job because this will not be an easy task. Networking may help if you can get options lined up. I would check with him to see if he would object to this first; it could be just a man thing.

Beware Of The Traps

Chapter 11

Beware Of The Traps

Beware Of The Traps

Beware Of The Traps

Some programs offer work-release programs where your son can be released temporarily throughout the day to go to work and may receive or earn passes to even come home to visit. It will be a reclamation period that will assist in the transitioning process into the real world. With this freedom comes responsibility.

The System Is Designed for Failure

To be placed in this work-release program, your son will be charged a rate for him to stay at this facility or group home. I call it rent. Therefore, if your son is being housed at a facility, there will be a daily fee for him to live there so it is encouraged that he goes out and finds a job very quickly. If he does not find a job quickly, facilities have the option to bill him. Be mindful if there are stipulations that if your son is out for too long without a job, he can be required to return to incarceration.

Keep in mind, being released with all the stipulations attached to it, can be a beautiful wrapping of a trap. The system is set up and designed for failure. The correctional facility is a huge money-making business. The facilities are built for a reason and someone has to house them. There is cheap labor internally, but external jobs are at stake that includes companies who supply the demands of the facilities, not to mention all the alleged illegal activity under the table and politics involved that is real.

In Ashely Black (2015) wrote an article entitled: Here are 6 Companies That Get Rich off Prisoners in Feb. 2015 in which she identified two of the companies getting rich off prisoners, Corrections Corporation of America (CCA) and the GEO Group (Private Prisons). She went on to say:

"The for-profit prison industry is worth $70 billion. Private prison companies like CCA and The Geo Group approach cash-strapped states and offer to save them money by buying their prisons. However, evidence that private prisons save money is mixed at best. States pay a daily fee for each prisoner housed in a private prisons, and corporations set a number of beds (usually no less than 1,000) and an occupancy rate (usually around 90 percent) that states must meet or pay a fine for each empty bed. It is unbelievable that such deals are legal since they give states an incentive, other than crime, to keep people in prison. In order to increase profit margins, private prisons keep prisoners in less humane and less sanitary conditions. This leads to higher incidences of violence, and higher rates of recidivism in private versus state-run prisons.

Beware Of The Traps

For-profit prison corporations also contribute to political campaigns and lobby states and the federal government to pass laws that will increase their profits. In the past 10 years, CCA has spent

$17.4 million on lobbying. Between 2003 and 2012, it made $1.9 million in political contributions. The Geo Group spent $2.5 million on lobbying in the last 8 years and $2.9 million in political contributions between 2003 and 2012. They help to write laws that create more prisoners. Two key methods are criminalizing more activities and increasing sentencing."

I caution your son to be aware of the traps set before him. If he's going to work off-site, be sure that he knows what the rules are and to follow them. He can be successful, however, breaking the rules is why he's in this predicament and that's what they are counting on to keep him there.

Trap #1: Probation

After your son has served his time within the facility and it is time for him to be released, more often than not, the court will establish a probationary period whereby he is on probation for 6-months, a year or 2 years, whatever the judge indicated at the initial sentencing. This means, your son cannot get into any trouble with the law during this period of time or he will get sent back to jail for the full term of the offense. For an example, if it is a state offense, he will be informed of the full sentence during the initial hearing; let's say it is a 4-years sentence, he may only serve 2. If he violates, he may have to return for the additional 2 years.

Probation means that there are still strict rules. It will be up to your son to find out the specifics of the probation as they vary. Changes can be made at a moment's notice so find out anything you don't understand from your attorney. It is important that your son follows suit and stay within the confines outlined in the specifics of what the probation entails for him. If the courts indicate that he can only go to work and or take a class, then work and school it will be.

Keep in mind, being on probation will not be easy. It will be up to him to succeed so it is important for him to have a clear understanding of what the sanctions are prior to release. In my situation, I knew my son was coming home to our family, so I wanted to be just as informed as to what the probation protocols entailed so that I knew how to support him. I wanted him to succeed. I didn't believe he had everything figured out yet as it related to direction, so I was concerned. He needed to be on time everywhere and that was unusual for me. Although the system is designed for failure, it is possible to pass the probationary period. Your son has to have the mindset that he will make it happen.

Readjusting to Life on the Outside

By no means will probation be an easy task. If you left your house for three weeks and returned, it will take time to get acclimated to familiar surroundings once you've been gone for a while. Your son will face the same dilemma times ten when he comes home. You are just not use to seeing your son home and he is not used to being there. This adjustment will not only be limited to his home environment, but the people he lives with, friends and family visiting.

Things that most people take for granted are foreign when you've been away for a while depending on how long you've been gone. It complicates matters even more when the environment that your son returns to is not conducive for him trying to better himself. What if the environment or his peers are the very thing that got him locked up in the first place? It is issues like this that need to be discussed and a plan developed of how to approach circumstances like this in advance. If he does not have a plan in his mind of how to address these negative determinants and distractions, he's setting himself up for failure. The definition of insanity is doing the same thing over and over and expecting a different outcome. He needs to figure out what he will do differently so that he doesn't violate his probation. This is crucial to the success of his probationary period. He needs to determine and ask himself the hard questions:

- What are my triggers?
- What needs to change prior to my coming home?
- Do I need to change my circle of friends? If so, who needs to be removed?
- Who is good for me to interact with?
- Who would be a good influence on me?
- Who has a bad influence on me?
- What do I need to do to ensure that I don't end up incarcerated again?
- What are some small steps that I can take to ensure that I get there?

Some things we can do for him but at some point, he has to take full responsibility for his actions. You will not be there with every waking moment of his life. He has to value his life for himself. It is natural and normal in this probationary period for you to be on pins and needles because you love him. But he has to mature, he has to grow up and he has to want this for himself. This is a decision that he's making about his life and he has to want it more than you want it for him.

Probation is not set up to be easy. Society is not forgiving or receptive of those who have made poor choices in their youth well into their adulthood. On the news, if something bad happens, the first thing they publicize is if the suspect had a previous run-in with the law. There's a negative stigma associated with first-time offenders and career criminals alike. Your son just needs to understand the vulnerability of the situation he's in now and do whatever it takes to get off probation.

Expungement

Since society is not so forgiving, some states have formulated expungement laws. This means that your son can have his record erased or removed completely if he qualifies after serving his time and remaining in good standing with the law over a certain period of time. Each state may vary so it would be worth checking to see what the rules and regulations are for your state and if what your state offers is applicable to your situation.

Trap #2: Meetings With The Probation Officer (PO)

There will be scheduled times when he will have to meet with his Probation Officer (PO). This scheduled meeting is mandatory for him to attend and he cannot be late. It is up to the PO when this meeting will take place. The PO is basically checking up on him to see what's going on to find out where his head is in this process. The PO has the right to make recommendations to the court, so everything is documented. If your son is late multiple times to this meeting or perhaps he does not show at all for his appointment, the PO has the right to recommend to the court that his release be suspended and your son will have to spend the rest of the sentenced time incarcerated full-time at the facility. For your son to have a good relationship with his PO will only work in his favor in the long run.

Trap #3: Working Off-Site

When he goes out to work, he will still be under close scrutiny. He will have to notify the probation officer of his schedule prior to leaving the facility or group home. He will have to notify his boss of his current situation so that his employer will know that restrictions may apply as it relates to him working at his establishment. When he is scheduled to work, he is expected to do the task required by the job and report back to the facility. If your son is returning late for any reason, it will be logged, and this will be documented against him. The Department of Corrections is developing a paper trail and this paper trail will be utilized in the courtroom to send him back to a more restricted environment. Although he may (not) be allowed to slide or be late one time, keep in mind any violation can send him back.

Trap #4: Department Of Corrections Listed On His Credit Report

Now, once your son has successfully made it through probation, he will now have a record. With this record, it may be difficult for him to find a job because there is a question on most applications that inquire about a criminal record or offense. But more importantly, remember when I mentioned it was all about the money? Remember when I mentioned the system is set up for him to fail? After he's served time for the crime committed, all of the fees and charges that he's incurred with vendors or corporations contracted with the state during his incarceration, they now want their money. The corporations want their money for daily fees associated for wearing the ankle bracelet as well as the rent that he was being charged for staying at the facility or a group home where he was allowed to leave and go get a job. They want all of the fees that may have been affiliated with his incarceration which may easily be in the thousands. From the beginning, the system was never set up for your son to be in a position to make this kind of money to pay for his expenses while incarcerated. He was making pennies an hour, remember? However, it was a part of the system structure for your son to be billed astronomical amounts in fees charged by the designated companies that the facilities do business with for your son's essential needs knowing in advance that it would place your son in debt while he was incarcerated. Your son will now be required to pay this money or at least get on a payment plan.

Now that he's a free man, despite his predicament and his circumstances, just like most other companies, if he does not pay the money in a timely manner, it will be taken to the next level and placed on his credit report. I went to make a payment for my son, and I happened to inquire as to what would the consequences be if he couldn't make his payment. I was informed that it will be sent to collections and then placed on his credit. To make matters worse, she went on to inform me

Beware Of The Traps

that the term "Department of Corrections" will be affiliated with the unpaid account.

The long-term effect is that when something goes on your credit, it remains for years even after the bill has been paid. Long after he's been incarcerated, the system is still set up for him to fail financially. To circumvent this bill from going on his report, it is important to find out the balance once he has been released so that he will know what he owes. Find out where the payments are to be sent, establish a payment agreement at least, and make the payments small or large. Be consistent. If you are consistent, they may be willing to work with you. If too many payments are missed, it can then be sent to collections and thus effecting his credit.

Thank Him In Advance For The Deliverance

Chapter 12

Thank Him In Advance For The Deliverance

Thank Him In Advance For The Deliverance

Thank Him In Advance For The Deliverance

Weather you get the record expunge or not, only God can give deliverance. You don't want to keep going through the same situation over and over. You want God to work on His heart and his mind. These are things that only God can change. He uses people and circumstances to make His impact. You want a change to take place and everything starts in the mind. Let's face it, everything that you've tried before has not worked. Now that you have exhausted yourself, this was a good time for Him to step in and show out. He wants the glory and for you to see what He can do without your help. This included putting you in a position where you couldn't help. You needed to relinquish your power to the Higher Power in order to see real results.

I know this is hard for you, but things will get better. Your son is young and the way he thinks, his mindset has to change. He can't keep thinking the same thoughts that landed him in trouble and believe if he continues on the same path, things will change. That's insanity. Once his thinking changes, his actions will change automatically. Once his actions change, he learns what it takes to control his temptations. Once he acquires knowledge, the use of knowledge is power. You are seeking rehabilitation. You don't want to ever go through this predicament again, not just for you, but for your son and your

Thank Him In Advance For The Deliverance

family. Ask God to change your son's heart and mind. Thank Him now for the deliverance in advance. CLAIM IT! Claim it on behalf of your son.

You don't know what the outcome will be, but you know that He knows. This is where your trust in your Lord and Savior comes into play. You've trusted God all your life. You knew that you were always in His care. This is the time where you have to dig deep and know that despite the circumstances, your son's location may have changed, but God has not. You are still in His care. Ask for your son's covering, safety and protection. Trust that He's watching over your son and that somehow, He's going to get the glory out of this. You don't know how, but you have to trust and believe that God knows what He's doing… and He does. We may not like the "how" because it hurts but we have to trust that He has our best interest at heart. Sometimes, you probably find it hard to sleep at night but go to sleep. Why? Because He's up working on your behalf and there is no reason for the both of you to be up at the same time. He loves you and your son, believe me, His timing is perfect.

You can't see the end from the beginning, but God does. He already knows the outcome and His timing is still perfect so start thanking him now for what He's going to do! And know that it's going to be goooood. Live in expectation.

Thank Him In Advance For The Deliverance

Whenever His hands are on something, expect greatness. He is no mediocre God. Don't think small when your God is SO big. Claim all that you knew was in your son when he was a child. Nothing has changed because that's the same kid. He has made a few bad choices, but you know what you've instilled in him. It's still there so the outcome can still be great with God. Talk to your God and let Him know that your expectations still have not wavered. Why? Because God can do ANYTHING! Don't put a BIG God in a little box. Let Him be who He is... GOD! Thank Him for the outcome. Thank Him just for Being GOD.

When you need Him directly because you find yourself losing the awareness of His comfort, find the Word. Ask God for understanding to what you read. Let Him know you need Him now and you are seeking His face. Ask Him for wisdom so that in what you read; it can be applicable in your life because you need some relief. Follow this up with going to your church. If you didn't have a church home, find a church that speaks to your heart.

I remember going to church with a broken heart about my son's situation. I felt like a zombie. I don't even know how I was able to drive there. All the saints around me were praising the Lord but my heart hurt so bad, I couldn't speak. I loved to praise the Lord, but I couldn't praise Him that day. The pain

Thank Him In Advance For The Deliverance

filled my soul. There were no words for my mouth. All I could do was cry. I cry as I write this because I remember this pain like it was yesterday.

I had to depend on the Holy Spirit to praise God on my behalf and speak to God for me. I felt like shattered glass, just broken. Oh God, it hurt so much. I literally could not speak. If you are in this type of pain, know that He understands. He sees every tear and He feels the depth of your pain. Hold on. Hang in there. These are the times when you are being carried. God loves you despite the circumstances around you, He still loves you. Be strong and hang in there. Things will get better. Everything will be alright after a while. I assure you not one tear will be wasted.

28 And we know that all things work together for good to them that love God, to them who are the called according to his purpose

(Romans 8:28)".

When you are able, in your spirit, let Him know that you are there to tell Him, "Thank You" for how He's going to use this situation to turn things around for the better. Let Him know that you understand that only He has the power to do so.

Thank Him In Advance For The Deliverance

Tell God you need Him, and you just want to give Him the praise just for loving you the way He does.

Understand that God is the one that allows the storms to come and allows them to end in His timing. He's the one who created the earth and has the power to shift the earth's plain on land to make an earthquake or shift the earth out at sea to cause a tsunami. Have you ever been to the beach and looked out in amazement at the ocean water? Have you questioned how does the ocean water know their limitations as to how far it is allowed to come up on shore? With man-made lakes, they flood but the ocean waters stop at a designated perimeter. As deep as the ocean is, what makes the water stop at the shore? As deep as the ocean is, why won't the water spill over on land? That fascinates me. It's only God.

5 He set the earth on its foundations;

it can never be moved.

6 You covered it with the watery depths as with a garment; the waters stood above the mountains.

7 But at your rebuke the waters fled,

at the sound of your thunder they took to flight;

8 they flowed over the mountains,

they went down into the valleys,

Thank Him In Advance For The Deliverance

to the place you assigned for them.

9 You set a boundary they cannot cross;

never again will they cover the earth.

Psalms 104: 5-9

He has the power over all that live and dwell in the sea and on land. We serve a BIG God. Surely, your situation is something He can handle. Focus on God instead of your crisis and the pain. He is so much bigger than we give Him credit for, so we need to address Him as who He really is and with all the might that He carries. He is indeed God so thank Him just for being God because surely, He deserves the reverence.

It also helps to remember what He has brought you through before in the past. When you stop to think about how He has saved your life knowing that you should have been dead today, He saved you for a reason. He's not done with you. God is not done with your son. He is the only one that literally has the power to zap the breath out of you in your next sentence. So, with this time that He's given you, how are you going to use it?

This too shall pass. This pain won't be here always. We are in the midst of a storm but when the storm passes, what did we learn from it? It's time to think about this now by seeking the lessons so that we won't have to repeat the training. God loves us so much; He disciplines those He loves just like a good father would. He is Love. There is so much to be learned from Him.

Start Thanking Him For How He's Going To Use This Circumstance To Turn Things Around

In going through something as difficult as knowing that your child has been incarcerated, what we don't see is that this experience is changing you. You are becoming stronger and more importantly, it is improving your relationship with God. He is turning something bad into something good. He knows that something painful and hurtful today can very well be something positive tomorrow. He specializes in turning dirt into something beautiful. He's always utilized the dirt, and this is a dirty situation. Even though you can't see how this could possibly end on a good note, don't focus on the bad. Keeping your focus on Him is the key. The bigger the burden, the bigger the blessing.

Thank Him In Advance For The Deliverance

11 For I know the plans I have for you," declares the Lord, "plans to prosper you and not to harm you, plans to give you hope and a future. 12 Then you will call on me and come and pray to me, and I will listen to you. 13 You will seek me and find me when you seek me with all your heart."

Jeremiah 29: 11-13

Repeat this over and over. Meditate on it. When you have no idea what the future holds, you go back to what God says and hold Him to His word. He can do anything. Tell your son everything will be alright because He is supposed to have a hope and a future. How many men do you know who are now older can say they don't know how they made it through but here they are? Many of them can tell you they had a praying mother or a praying grandmother that they know was praying for them. Well, that's just a testament to what God can do. You intercede on the behalf of your son. Pray on their behalf because they need Him right now whether they know it or not. He hears everything you say to Him. He has the power to turn things around so ask Him.

View this crisis as an opportunity. It's all about perception. It's an opportunity for God to step in and show out so let Him. You are in a position to witness His power first hand. Be confident in knowing that God is doing a great thing in your son's life and tell others that the best is yet to come. God hears prayer but answers faith. He is watching your attitude. Don't feel like you're defeated because that is the trick of the enemy; defeated you are not. How can you be with God on your side? He has the last say so. It's okay if others think you've lost it, or they don't understand how you can walk in assurance. They are watching your walk now more than ever because pain has come to your house. They want to see how you will react and how you will handle adversity with your Godly self. The thing is, the blessing isn't just for you and your family. They will be a witness to the blessing as well. Years down the road, they will remember how you handled the situation and see the results of God's work. Remember, He has the last say. He is the living word. Nothing happens without His permission.

Spiritual Warfare

Chapter 13

Spiritual Warfare

Spiritual Warfare

Spiritual Warfare

Every day we live in this world watching what goes on around us as we exist; we see, touch and feel. But there is another spirit world that we rarely give thought to that we co-exist in around us as well. Angels are around us all the time and the Holy Spirit is the activity of God providing us with guidance and direction for our lives. But Satan is always busy and works hard to manipulate our minds to doing what is wrong. If we knew clearly right from wrong, it would be too easy to do the right thing, so the war isn't taking place externally, it begins in the mind. This is where the spiritual warfare takes place. It's the deception that you cannot see where the seed is sin is placed before we carry it out. It is then left up to us whether or not we nip it in the bud or allow this seed to grow.

You Can't Stay Angry So Use It to Make A Difference

Throughout this entire process, I encourage you to pray your way through it. Tell your Heavenly Father what you want and don't hold back. If you are angry, it's okay to let Him know; you are not the first and I'm sure you will not be the last. Let Him know that you want Satan to pay for messing with your son and your family. Satan chose to mess with your son's mind early because the goal was to get him young. Satan could see all that your son could grow up to become and was threatened.

Spiritual Warfare

Everything starts in the mind. If he could play with his mind, then he felt that he had him. He knew of the brilliance waiting in your son's future and how God could use him to make change in this world for the better. He knew that he had a lot of good to contribute. He knew that he could only uplift God's kingdom. So, he peaked into your son's future, saw the vision and felt that he had to do something before your son found out who he really belong to and was strategic in his approach. The goal was to destroy him early so that he would not reach his potential. What he didn't take into account was that he was messing with the wrong mother. This is the worst thing Satan could have done because now he's made you mad.

Nothing will get a parent going quicker than when you mess with one of their cubs. You tell God because no one can repay harm like God can. Don't you try to address the problem, turn it over to God, leave it at the throne and watch what God does. Let Him know that you want Satan to pay by allowing your child to excel much greater than the original vision for your son's life. Let Him know that for every tear that you've cried because of this incidence, you want joy. Let Him know that regardless of this circumstance, you want your son to become a preacher, a teacher, a doctor, a lawyer or whatever the blessing you've had in mind for him. This doesn't stop your

Spiritual Warfare

son's life. Your son may have taken a detour from his happiness, but his life is not over. Let Him know that you reject the gossip regarding your son of what he can't accomplish because of a record. God has the power to dismiss the record and if He so chooses, He has the power to leave the record as is and excel your son in spite of it.

Tell Him what Satan has done and tell Him what you want done about it and let the anger go. You are not to dwell there. Let Him know what you want and leave it on the table. God can do anything, so you don't have to worry about the how. You just live in expectation. Live in expectation of something GREAT! And if you really mean it, take it a step further and tell others about what God is going to do in spite of the circumstances. I still tell people you better look out for what my son is going to do. I refuse to underestimate my God. Knowing that, be sure that you are not thinking too small. Ask for the sun, the moon and the stars. He wants you to do this. He has it and He wants to give it to you. Turn that anger into something positive. Getting off my knees, lamenting to God, angry because Satan has hurt me, I'm going in HARD. I want Satan to know that He's messed with the wrong one and nobody will make this more evident than God stepping in to make it clear. So, tell Him all that you want to come from this and step back, give Him time and watch what He does. Ask Him to use you and channel this anger to make a difference.

Our Real State of the Union

As I contemplate on America, the land of the free and home of the brave, I question this freedom for black men in America when black men are so disproportionately represented in the criminal justice system. As our young black men leave their homes every day, are they really free when they are walking around with an invisible target on their backs and a countdown clock ticking before they too may be arrested? America are you really the home of the brave when you continue to historically abused power by repeatedly taking advantage of those who have the least. Cory Booker, a presidential candidate in the 2020 elections made a statement that has stuck with many people. He said,

"In America, you are treated better if you are rich and guilty than if you are poor and innocent."

I would take it a step further and say that America portrays this image that we are beautiful but our little secret is that we as a nation, was born with a major birth defect whereby the distortion is in the heart and the diagnosis is that we have a malignant disease called Racism and it is slowly killing us. Now what are we going to do about it? Ignoring it and allowing it to continue to spread generationally isn't working.

One of the most powerful documentaries I have ever seen is called the 13th (2016), directed by Ava DuVernay that speaks to the overlap of race, justice, and mass incarceration in America. She lays out the framework for how incarceration was a deliberate mechanism utilized to control black people and stipple their growth. The documentary explored the 13thAmendment to the United States Constitution which abolished slavery and followed the historical component of incarcerating black men to present day. There are so many black people incarcerated at alarming rates because it is part of America's design to take advantage of the most vulnerable. I commend Ava DuVernay and Oprah Winfrey for shedding a light on the history of the racial bias of black men disproportionally represented in our criminal justice system in America.

If you're ugly on the inside, it's going to eventually show on the outside. Families of color are being allowed by Americans to be ripped apart in present day and we are now exposed worldwide that we are not so beautiful after all. Now the world can see what's really in our hearts. We are a big melting pot of immigrants but even though the color of hate is now more dominant than the color of love, I have to believe love will somehow win. We went from having the best President to the worst. President Barack Obama was well loved not just in America, but on a worldwide level. His name symbolizes HOPE and UNITY. I can't mention him without mentioning his wife Michelle Obama. She symbolized STRENGTH and DIGNITY. They will forever be remembered for the class and poise they represented while in office. In stark contrast, we now have a man in office who will be remembered as the worst president in modern day history whose name symbolizes HATE and DIVISION sadly on a global scale. He has admitted to being a white nationalist/supremacist and some 38% of the country still support him. Since he's been elected, hate crimes around the world are increasing and hate crimes in the United States alone has increased 70%. Since the racism is killing us at our core, can we talk about our disfunction? Ignoring it isn't working so let's have an honest conversation.

The criminal justice system is a symbol of the hate and prejudice in this country. We are the world's leader in incarcerating our citizens. Now we are looking at people of color fleeing their country because they choose life for themselves and their children. Regardless of color, it takes a lot of hate and fear to rip a baby from the mother and you sleep at night without a conscious. All of these beautiful human beings who needed our help were having their families separated because there were too many of them fleeing for their lives at once and because they are people of color. Once they set foot on American soil, the men are immediately registered into the criminal justice system and sent on the fast track to be returned to the country of which they fled. Whenever they do return to America for any reason, they already have a criminal record. There are a few select white people in power who are once again making the decision to rip families apart that don't look like them. America, does this feel like déjà vu to you at all? History is repeating itself once again with people of color. Many of those small children taken from their parents were transported all over America, placed in foster care and have already been adopted. What happens to the adopted parents of those children when the child wants to find their birth parents and they've grown attached. What about the children? God sees all. I challenge America with all of its advanced technology to develop a method to trace ancestral DNA specifically for these children in effort for them to have an opportunity to reconnect to their families at some point in time.

Spiritual Warfare

When I was a child, I went to school every day and before class started at the beginning of each morning, we all stood up to face the American flag, and placed our hands over our hearts and stated our Pledge of Allegiance. I remember, it always ended … "with liberty and justice for all." I didn't realize that sadly our pledge should have been more specific, and we should have been saying "with liberty and equal justice for all". Now that I'm older, it has become painfully clear that rich people can afford the defense, so they often serve very little time, get probation or walk and serve no time at all. The problem with this is when justice has an economic component or a race component or a class component, then it's not really justice at all.

Lessons Learned

Lessons Learned

Chapter 14

Lessons Learned

Lessons Learned

Lessons Learned

I Learned... The Significance of Learning the Miranda Warning

It would be advantages to learn the Miranda Warning and what they mean for you. It will be beneficial so that you are knowledgeable about what your rights are in advance and then to educate your children.

My Recommendation:

One of the most important warnings that authorities give to your son is that he is warned that a confession at the time of the scene can be used against him in court. What happens at the scene is critical to the outcome of your son's defense, so the use of knowledge is power. Let him know that he is to verbally request to speak with his attorney and to provide no information.

I Learned... The Juvenile System Can Provide Assistance to Those in Need.

The juvenile system should not be a precursor for the adult system. I learned that if you are a parent and your son has violated the law, the juvenile system is there with the purpose to provide the assistance to the family if they need it. You are

Lessons Learned

perfectly within your rights to ask the court for assistance during this difficult time of rearing your son.

I asked one of the judges for assistance and he instructed me to "Ground your son and take the locks off his bedroom door so that he could not lock his door or take the door off the hinge; it's your house anyways". I respectfully informed him, "I can ground my son, remove the locks and the door for that matter but that does not address the real problem here. I need help!"

The courts ended up providing my family with mandatory counseling by having a pastor of my choosing who was also a therapist come by my house for family counseling as a part of my son's probation upon release. I encourage you to request that the court work "with" you to get you the help you need.

My Recommendation:

Listen and be ready. Get in the habit of being prepared to use your voice and speaking up. If you find that you've come across a judge that will work with you, take advantage of it while the judge is in front of you and particularly, if he's offering. Keep in mind, the Prosecutor's Office will fight you all the way. Nonetheless, before you get a judge who is just

Lessons Learned

doing "a job", work with a judge whenever you can. At the end of the day, no one can advocate for your son better than you.

I can recall having a private attorney at one point and saw her going back and forth with the Prosecutor's office during one of the hearings. By this time, I had spoken in front of the judge on my son's behalf so much until the judges learned who I was, and they expected to hear what I had to say knowing I wanted to contribute to the discussion. If you respect the court, speak well and articulate your concern on behalf of your son. Your voice will carry weight. Listen to what is being said in the courtroom and be prepared to advocate for your son each time you go to court.

I Learned...To Listen to My Son

As the public defenders vary with time, my son was still in juvey with all the other young men. Many of them had been there before in and out of the system. Some of the other young men are familiar with the public defenders and will educate your son on who will work in his best interest and who will not. They discuss this information among themselves so if your son provides you information on the various public defenders, his recommendations are from good sources.

Lessons Learned

My Recommendation:

Give more weight to what he's telling you and adhere to his wishes, besides, it is his life. Listen and believe what your son is telling you from his resources and take his advice. It may be that an attorney is portraying to be a good attorney to me as a parent, but your son's peers know better. Take serious consideration to all of his recommendations.

I Learned... Just How Much They Are Getting Behind in School when Incarcerated

The Juvenile Detention Center is being utilized as a system similar to that of the approach schools utilize of placing kids in detention. Many students are not getting premium class instruction and there is no "real" benefit other than taking the kids off the streets or temporarily removing them from the home. Day in and day out the kids just sit and wait for their hearing left to wonder what will happen. Their primary desire that is first and foremost in their minds is that that they all want out of juvey. Not all want to go home but they all want out of juvey. Nobody wants to sit around most of the day in one room.

Lessons Learned

Many of our youth of promise who are incarcerated have previously had problems in school by being disruptive in the classroom in some form. My son had been suspended often and ultimately expelled from school. This was added pressure because if you are in middle school or high school and you are not doing well, it is depressing, and it can show its face in many ways. When you start to see life spiraling out of control, it's like quicksand when bad decisions are being made on a continuous basis.

My Recommendation:

This is where I would like to see our juvenile centers step up to the plate to save our youth. When they are brought to the juvenile detention center, risk assessment can be taken in effort to obtain the necessary data to determine if a child has a high, medium or low risk of being a repeat offender and have a planned implementation of services readily available.

I Learned... Programs May Be Outdated

There are various programs offered that I'm sure are great programs, but I question the effectiveness of the programs. I cannot comfortably say that I am secure that the needs are being met for these young men.

Lessons Learned

My Recommendation:

I would suggest that the Office of Juvenile Justice and Delinquency Prevention (OJJDP) at the federal level develop standardized protocols and assessments to monitor the overall effectiveness of the juvenile detention centers.

All juvenile detention center programs that are being offered should be regularly monitored, evaluated, and held accountable on a regular basis to determine the efficacy of the programs offered. This can be implemented by conducting assessments on these programs on an annual basis to determine the strengths and weaknesses of each juvenile detention center. This documentation can then be utilized to determine if you just have programs that have existed for over the last 20 years but are not meeting the needs of the youth of promise or if they are programs that are actually making a difference.

I would also incorporate programs that address not only the problem that led to them being placed in juvey but the core of the problem so that the young men won't return. While the juvenile detention center has these young men in their possession with all this free time, why not take advantage of this critical time to do the real work that needs to be done to reach them.

Lessons Learned

To give an analogy, currently it's like seeing a young man physically cut and bleeding from a deep wound. We get him to the emergency room of the hospital, and the physician applies a band aid and sends him home. We haven't addressed the real issue so there is a real probability that they will return. The wound has not been addressed. By the mere fact that they are in juvey, it is a cry for help. As a society, we need to be more productive with the time that we have with them to make a real difference.

I Learned… It's All About That Dollar Bill

"Money is a huge reason we have so many prisoners. Several corporations make huge profits off prisons. It costs an average of $23,876 annually to house a state prisoner for a year. To save money, cash-strapped states (aka, us, the taxpayers) pay companies to deal with their prisoners.

Companies make money by running prisons as cheaply as possible and squeezing prisoners and their families for money for basic necessities and fees. As a result, private prisons are a $70 billion industry.

Even crazier, 65 percent of private prison contracts require an occupancy guarantee. That means states must have a certain amount of prisoners — typically between 80 and 90 percent of occupancy — or pay companies for empty beds." says Ashely Black (2015)

Lessons Learned

At the end of the day, money talks and image gets to walk. Sadly, it's all about that dollar bill in the courtroom. Money, status and power in that courtroom is huge leverage.

My Recommendation:

We need criminal justice reformation... bad. This would include new policy development that includes multiple levels of accountability from the judges, to law enforcement to personnel staff. Greater accountability would include incorporating a Civilian Review Board so that citizens would be a part of the decision-making process. The current system is embarrassing and shameful.

In addition, there should also be Law Enforcement Reform as well. If we are navigating our society to adapt to community policing, then why is law enforcement making their own rules for what happens with their employees in bad incidences without citizen input? This too is shameful. If something happens like a shooting in our communities that include law enforcement, in most cases, the officer is automatically placed on administrative leave until the investigation is complete. The problem with this is (1) the media has stopped reporting that the officers on administrative leave are actually on "PAID" administrative leave (2) citizens in many states are not on the Review Board that makes the determination of the final outcomes of the cases and (3) in some states, the officers who are reprimanded are allowed to go to the next county to continue working so there are no permanent consequences.

Too often, a family is told, "I'm sorry." Yet, if you do something stupid on your job, you don't have the luxury of a paid grace period until your investigation complete. This is unacceptable. Community policing should work both ways. The community representation should be included at the table with police in the decision-making process as it relates to fair disciplinary actions.

I Learned...There Are Not Enough Mental Health Resources Available.

When our sons are not being targeted and they need our help, we need the resources made available to get them the help they need. Money isn't well spent on prevention of youth of promise from entering the criminal justice systems. Everything that exist in our society today started with an idea. This idea was preceded with actions based off of our thought process. Our behaviors and actions are therefore a direct result of our thinking. The behavior of our youth of promise is a direct result of their thought processes bad or good. The battle is in the mind.

If we focused more attention on addressing the mental health issues of not only adults but our children and addressing those needs early, our country can produce healthier adults who can make a significant contribution to our society. Our youth are SCREAMING for help, but many voices go unheard. Instead, we lock them up and do not provide the effective services they need. We then release them back into society unprepared and unequipped to handle the pressures and stresses that life brings. A child with mental health issues grows up to become an adult with mental health issues if the concerns are not addressed early.

My Recommendations:

If we are serious about criminal justice reformation, addressing mental health concerns is just a start. Why are we being reactive instead of proactive? With all the funds allocated in budgets for the system, this is where additional funding can be reallocated to hire psychological services to address the needs of the youth. The difference that should be incorporated with the reformation process is that there is a Quality Assurance Division that conducts evaluations on services

Lessons Learned

provided in all areas. Most companies have a division who oversee accountability. There should be data submitted so that we can visually see if services provided are successful. If not, determine what needs to change and make the change. Re-evaluating and improving services again should be the norm. Monitoring the youth by offering additional services once they are released and collecting the data to see if there is a decline in recidivism will play a role as this data will define success. If we are serious about criminal justice reformation, there are many ways of approach but are we willing make the changes that need to be made to show our youth that we really do care, or will we continue to "talk" about it is yet to be determined.

In December 2018, the U.S. Congress passed the First Step Act with the support of private prison giants. The Geo Group and CoreCivic/Avalon have been identified in the report previously mentioned by Worth Rises (2109) as private companies who will still benefit. My recommendation is to find out if companies you support are on this list of 4000 for-profit companies and make a judgement call if you still want to support their services.

I Learned... That the sentencing chart rules (depending on who you are or who you know)

Lessons Learned

There was one time in particular that stands out when the judge had to backtrack her decision due to mandatory sentencing. I learned each individual and their case is different and brings with them a different story, however in court, from my perspective the individuals are now only their assigned numbers. In court, the stories quickly became irrelevant. All that mattered was what was written on that sentencing chart. After listening to the public defender present my son's case and after comparing it to the state's defense, she had made a ruling that would have favored my son to his advantage. However, the state's Prosecuting Attorney reminded her that a new rule had just passed some 3 weeks earlier and based on the new rule, she had to go in a different direction that meant mandatory sentencing for my son. I was confused because I thought that was the purpose of the judge to provide the final decision until I later learned about the nature of how the biased is infiltrated throughout the judicial system.

For instance, in 2015, you have a white male who is a college student, Brock Turner, attending Stanford University and he is convicted of 3 counts of felony sexual assault on an unconscious woman who was later found behind a dumpster in California. His attorney pleaded with the court that he was a good kid and we didn't want to mess up is college opportunity.

Lessons Learned

Prosecutors argued that according to the sentencing chart that indicated a range of 2-14 years for his charges, Turner should get a minimum 6-year sentence in the state prison for his felony. Instead, the judge accepted the recommendation from Turner's lawyer that due to his lack of criminal history, his "sincere remorse" and alcohol involvement, it impaired Turner's judgement. Brock Turner was sentenced to a 6-month sentence in a "county" jail and served 3 months due to good behavior never seeing a prison door. There are too many cases to name where the color of your skin or how wealthy you were, benefited or hurt you in the court room.

My Recommendation:

ELIMINATE MANDATORY SENTENCING!!! If we are going to take into account situational circumstances, then everyone should have the same opportunity. Anything less than what is fair, is unjust and unacceptable. Additionally, if your son is to be jailed according to what is predetermined on a sentencing chart, then why is Brock Turner's sentence legal?

It's Time to Dance

Chapter 15

It's Time to Dance

It's Time to Dance

It's Time to Dance

My son had successfully completed his probation and was working odd jobs here and there. He had also enrolled in the local community college. He was clearly still struggling, and I could tell he wasn't happy. I couldn't remember the last time I had seen him smile. Although I'm sure he was glad to be home, he despised being back in the same environment where his life initially changed for the worse but knew he needed to live at home for a while to regroup. I remember being fearful for him every time he left the house. I felt like he was a target to police if he was stopped; as a man with a record he could be arrested again just because. But God.

He was trying his best to do everything he could to get himself together. All the while my oldest daughter was off in college throughout this entire process and mentally this was a lot on our family including her. My prayer for her was that this situation with my son would not affect her studies. She called me one day from school in Washington, DC to inquire about her brother asking how he was doing. I told her he was coming along. She then asked me, "Well, I asked because the fall classes here will be starting in about 6 weeks or so and I wanted to know how you felt about him going to school here?" I initially was taken back but as I listened to her, I could hear God was speaking through her; using her as a blessing. She explained how she lived next door to the community college there, he could get an apartment in her building and go off to college and be on his own. I cried when I hung up the phone.

I didn't want to get his hopes up without doing some investigating first. I called my daughter's apartment manager; we had a good relationship. The apartment set up was that you were renting rooms with a common area for the living room and kitchen. She inquired did he want the smaller room with a shower or the room with a full bathroom with a tub? I told her the larger room where he could take a bath whenever he'd like simply since it hadn't been an option for so long. She informed me that she had a room available that met his needs, but she needed him to submit an application as soon as possible because they were the first to go and they were filling up due to the upcoming semester. However, she confirmed that it was doable on her end and she would look for his application, but she basically told me he had it.

When he came home, I told him I needed to talk to him. I explained all that had happened that day. He showed no reaction, just hollow on the inside because it just sound too unbelievable for him. He said, "Sure I would like to go." I could tell he wasn't going to allow his hopes to get up. I was reminded of all the times I kept reiterating to him in so many of my letters over and over again while he was away,

It's Time to Dance

11 For I know the plans I have for you," declares the Lord, "plans to prosper you and not to harm you, plans to give you hope and a future (Jeremiah 29:11).

We first googled her apartment complex and he completed the apartment application. Then he googled the school and we paid the fee for the online application and proceeded to complete his school application. Two days later, he was accepted into school and they sent him a Student ID number. The next day, the emails began. They were emailing him utilizing his Student ID number asking for his FASFA, and then to take a Placement Test, and then a notice to meet with your Academic Advisor and then a School Alert. Every time we looked up, there was another email for this and that back to back. Oh my God it was happening. You could see God's hand and He was swift. We then completed the FASFA (Free Application for Federal Student Aid) and he took a Placement Test to see what classes he could take. He then received approval to register for classes. We were blown away at how fast God was moving.

I had already planned to go and visit my daughter and while I was there, I had a meeting with the apartment manager to discuss his room. I wanted to make sure all of the T's were crossed and the I's were dotted. While there, she waived his application fee and accommodated him on everything with his application with the exception of his request to be on a floor with all females. She told me to tell him, "Nice try…it's not happening." We were able to solidify his room and board by the end of the meeting. He was set. I returned home with the news and I could tell he was still in disbelief. He had to see it to belief it. I overheard him on the phone talking to someone about going off to school and he told them, "It would have to be a miracle." My heart moved because I wanted it bad for him and for him to see that it was just that; a miracle that only God can do.

My daughter flew in before school started but this trip would be different. When she left this time, it was to take her brother back with her. Their building had 16 floors. She lived on the 13th floor in a larger room and now he would be moving to the 8th floor larger room. Their building had a state-of-the-art gym and a computer room on the main level. What blew me away was that on the top floor of the building, there was a rooftop swimming pool and you could look out over the city. Outside to the left of their building was a movie theatre adjacent to a soul food restaurant with a mall across the street. I was thankful to God that He had set them up to live in a very nice environment. My son could see other young men who looked and behaved like him, but they were in school working

It's Time to Dance

towards a goal. Everyone in his environment was striving to become something with their life including his biggest support system, his sister. I felt comfort knowing that they were there for each other. If one ran out of food like college kids do, they had each other covered. That's college life.

Weeks had past and it was time for them to leave. I held it together but cried privately. I was just so grateful that the day had come when this chapter was over. I took them to the airport and fought back the tears as I hugged my children good-bye. My daughter was her happy-go-lucky self as usual making jokes repeatedly asking me if I was okay. "Yes, I'm fine" as I lied repeatedly. My son was just going along for the ride not knowing what to expect. I think maybe it was starting to set in that this really is happening. I will never forget seeing them walk through the doors of the airport with their backs facing me as my son walked into the next chapter of his life. Wow… I cried full throttle when I made it back to the car. I mean I let her rip! I thought of everything that we had been through to get us to this point. I thought of the countless prayers and now my prayers were being answered in a way I could never have planned myself. My daughter later told me that when they got on the plane, when it came time for take-off, my son lost his cool as he could feel the strong vibrations of the engine slowly begin to increase. She had the window seat and it had never dawned on her that this was the first time he had ever rode on a plane. She said he was grinning from ear to ear.

What a way to start a new life.

"And we know that all things work together for good to those who love God, to those who are the called according to His purpose."

Romans 8:28.

References

References

References

References:

http://federaldrugcharges.net/topics/what-you-should-know-if-youve-been-arrested-on-drug-charges/

http://www.indy.gov/eGov/Council/Committees/Pages/Re-Entry-Study-Commission.aspx

http://www.indy.gov/eGov/Council/Committees/Documents/RE-ENTRY/Meeting%20Five/Notes%20from%20the%20Marion%20County%20Re-Entry%20Coalition.pdf

http://www.indy.gov/egov/council/committees/documents/re-entry/re-entry%20policy%20report.pdf

Book: Graph applicable; A study conducted, Page 15- 16 & Page 44

http://www.mirandawarning.org/whatareyourmirandarights.html

Carlton, Genevieve (2018), 50 Large American Companies That Use Prison Labor

References

http://www.indy.gov/egov/council/committees/documents/re-entry/re-entry%20HYPERLINK-

"http://www.indy.gov/egov/council/committees/documents/re-entry/re-entry%20policy%20report.pdf"policy%20report.pdf

http://www.indianahelpers.com/Presentations_Other/Marys_MarionCountyStatus.pdf

http://csgjusticecenter.org/nrrc/posts/indianapolis-business-leaders-discuss-hiring-individuals-with-criminal-records/

http://www.mirandawarning.org/whatareyourmirandarights.html

Retrieved on August 18, 2015 from

http://criminal.findlaw.com/criminal-procedure/plea-bargain.html

http://www.indy.gov/egov/council/committees/documents/re-entry/re-entry%20policy%20report.pdf

Retrieved on January 12, 2015 from:

References

http://criminal.findlaw.com/criminal-procedure/plea-bargain.html

http://www.indy.gov/egov/council/committees/documents/re-entry/re-entry%20policy%20report.pdf

Retrieved on January 12, 2015 from:
http://criminal.findlaw.com/criminal-charges/view-all-criminal-charges.html

Retrieved on June 13, 2015 from:
http://www.criminaldefenselawyer.com/resources/criminal-defense/felony-offense/indiana-felony-class.htm

Retrieved on June 13, 2015 from:
http://www.criminaldefenselawyer.com/resources/indiana-misdemeanor-crimes-class-and-sentences.htm

http://federaldrugcharges.net/topics/what-you-should-know-if-youve-been-arrested-on-drug-charges/

"http://www.myindianadefenselawyer.com/criminal-charges/".myindianadefenselawyer.com/criminal-charges/

http://www.cnn.com/2016/09/06/us/brock-turner-sex-offender-registry/

References

Iyanla Vanzant, Until Today, Daily Devotions for Spiritual Growth and Peace of Mind. (2000) Simon & Schuster

http://biblehub.com/proverbs/27-10.htm

Retrieved 8-8-2016 from

http://www.attn.com/stories/941/who-profits-from- prisoners

5-10 year HYPERLINK "http://mic.com/articles/86519/19-actual-statistics-about-america-s-prison-system"s)

Here are 6 Companies That Get Rich off Prisoners by: Ashley Nicole Black @ ASHLEYN1COLE Feb. 21, 2015

http://time.com/3446372/criminal-justice-prisoners-profit/

https://theintercept.com/2019/04/02/connecticut-free-prison-calls/

https://worthrises.org/picreport2019

"http://time.com/3446372/criminal-justice-prisoners-profit/"prisoners and their families for money for

References

https://www.ranker.com/list/companies-in-the-united-states-that-use-prison-labor/genevieve-carlton

References

www.ingramcontent.com/pod-product-compliance
Lightning Source LLC
Chambersburg PA
CBHW051048160426
43193CB00010B/1111